Siren of the Heart

■

SIREN

of the

HEART

selected poems by

GAD BEN-MEIR

■

Westphalia Press
An Imprint of the Policy Studies Organization
Washington, DC
2020

SIREN OF THE HEART
All Rights Reserved © 2020 by Policy Studies Organization

Westphalia Press
An imprint of Policy Studies Organization
1527 New Hampshire Ave., NW
Washington, D.C. 20036
info@ipsonet.org

ISBN-10: 1-63391-826-2
ISBN-13: 978-1-63391-826-9

Cover and interior design by Jeffrey Barnes
jbarnesbook.design

Daniel Gutierrez-Sandoval, Executive Director
PSO and Westphalia Press

Updated material and comments on this edition
can be found at the Westphalia Press website:
www.westphaliapress.org

DEDICATION

To my dear wife Judith and
my sons, Doron and Michael.
With my love and gratitude.

BYRON TO APHRODITE

Table of Contents

REFLECTIONS

LAMENTATIONS

INTRODUCTION

*(by Lev Hakak, Ph.D., Prof. of Hebrew Language and
Literature, University of California, Los Angeles, USA)*

Biographical Notes About the Author

The life of Gad Ben-Meir, LL.B, LL.M is rich with activity and achievements. It is a combination of intellectual and spiritual achievements with attention to practicality. The life axes of the author are family, intellectual, spiritual accomplishments and public service. It is a distinguished, intense life.

Gad's life story has roots in four countries (Iraq, Israel, England and Australia), and in each of them he shined in both communal service and personal achievement.

Gad was born in Baghdad in 1931. He received his primary education in a State school and his secondary education in a Jewish school. Upon graduation in 1947 he served as a teacher at the Alliance Israelite Univercelle in Baghdad. In 1950 he and his family migrated to Israel. He studied law at the Hebrew University in Jerusalem and graduated with LL.M. Degree in 1955. During his studies he served the compulsory two years in the Israeli Defence Force.

After doing two years articles at a Lawyer's office in Tel-Aviv, Gad was admitted to the Israeli Bar in 1957 and practiced law in Tel-Aviv for a short while. He later joined the Arab Department of the General Federation of Labour ("Histadrut") and was involved in the economic development of the Arab Sector. He also served as the Editor of *Al-Ta'awun* (Co-operation), a monthly magazine published in Arabic by his Department. In those years, he established himself as an important professional who made meaningful contributions to the economic and political advancement of the Arab minority in Israel. He was also active in Israeli party politics as well as the Tel-Aviv Bar Association.

In 1965, Gad was appointed as the Executive Director of the World Sephardi Federation (WSF) in London, working with then President Denzil Sebag Montefiore and representing the WSF in a number of Jewish and Zionist congresses. He wrote articles on Jewish and Middle Eastern affairs in the WSF's bi-monthly, *Sepharad*, and in other local Jewish publications. In July, 1963 he married his Manchester-born wife, Judith Cohen in London. Together they had two sons, Doron, born in 1965, and Michael, born in 1970, and one daughter, Tania, born in 1966.

In 1968, Gad and his family migrated to Australia where Judith's parents had settled back in 1948. He initially went into business and, nine years later, enrolled at Monash University, obtained his LL.B. degree and was admitted as Barrister and Solicitor of the Supreme Court of Victoria in February 1979 and practiced law until his retirement in July 2017.

Gad had a lengthy involvement in Victorian State Politics and Jewish Communal Affairs. He became President of the Sephardi Association of Victoria, and built the first Sephardi Synagogue in that State. He invited the late Mr. Malcolm Fraser, then Prime Minister of Australia, to officially open the Synagogue and again to celebrate its 10th Anniversary.

Gad served for 5 years as Chairman of the Australian Friends of Tel Aviv University (TAU), for 8 years as Editor of its Annual Magazine, *ALEPH-TAV*, and still serves as a member of its Board of Governors. He represented the Victorian Sephardi Community at the Jewish Council of Victoria for a few years and for 13 years acted as Editor of *Gesher*, the annual publication of the Victorian Council of Christians and Jews.

Gad also served as the Victorian and then Federal President of Jewish Ex-Servicemen & Women, as Chairman of the Victorian Inner Eastern Regional Consultative Council, as Vice President of the Wheelers Hill Branch of the Liberal Party, as President of its Middle Camberwell Branch, as President of the Liberal

Speakers Group, as Executive Member of the Hawthorn Electorate Council and a Delegate to Liberal Party State Conferences.

Gad has been enamoured with Arabic poetry since his secondary schooling at Shammash Secondary School in Baghdad. He published some of his work in *Kalimat*, bi-annual periodical published (but no longer) in Sydney, Australia under the editorship of Mr. Raghid Nahhas, originally from Syria.

During the years of his treasured friendship with the late Prof. Shmuel Moreh, then President of the Association of Jewish Academics from Iraq and the winner of the Israel Prize, Prof. Moreh energized Gad's love for poetry writing. As a result, Gad published two poetry books in 2004: *The Nightingales of Intimacy*, in literal Arabic, and *Ya Manal Ya Manali*, in the Egyptian dialect. Prof. Moreh wrote the foreword for both as he did in 2008 for Gad's third poetry book *Dialogue of the Hearts*, also in literal Arabic.

Notes About the Poems in this Book

After about 54 years of living in English-speaking countries, in this work, Gad presents poems he wrote in English. He divided his poems into several sections that reveal the focal points of his spiritual life. His poems revolve primarily on love, with all its ups and downs, and including sections: Reflections, Celebrations, Lamentations and Condolences.

Here's an excerpt of the poem *"Life and Love"* which is, in many ways, typical of Gad's poetic bent when he says:

> I bask with those who smile
> And shun all those who frown
> 'Cause life is only a while
> And love its glorious crown.

Love never stays still
Make lovers rise uphill
Bubbly and fresh
In spirit and flesh,

Row leisurely, you lucky lovers,
Your hearts shall dance, new passion discover
Where the sun shines and the moon smiles
And you remain entranced, for long, long whiles.

Or when love's allusions are shattered and the spell of fancy broken Gad's poem "*Nightly Tears*" tackles the resulting feelings:

She lives her daily dramas
And sheds her nightly tears
Adrift with shattered allusions
With heart enmeshed in fears.
With the spell of her fancy broken
And her lust for loving ensnared
She lost her romantic token
And the fire within despaired.

But when a storm clips a few feathers from love's wings, Gad comforts the lovers in "*Love, a Bird with Wondrous Wings*" where he says:

Love is a bird with wondrous wings
Gently perches on the soul,
Sings the wordless tune
And heeds the lovers' call.

A storm may clip a sore few
Feathers from its caressing wings

Yet sweet remains the flowing dew
With the fragrance of its living springs.

The Condolences section includes the eulogy of Gad's dear
Mother, Yaffa. Here's an extract:

We all reach the end of living
Some sighing the hymns of despair
Others the hope of fresh beginning
In a cradle breathing their mother's love.
I imagine the days ahead
And see your roses bloom,
Feel your love like a small sun
Warming the turrets and vales of my life and
Breathing the perfume
Reeking from your soul
Till ... my ... heart ... ceases ... to ... beat.

His poem eulogising his dear friend, the late Prof. Shmuel
Moreh (who was also a friend of mine) I find deeply touching.
Here's an excerpt:

You loved life with its smiles and tears
And excelled as poet and outstanding scholar;
The praise of your achievements you cannot hear
Time cannot efface, nor the seasons wither.
Shame such smiling eyes go under the earth's lid
And the sparks of ebullient talent fade away;
But your smiling soul, your loving heart, the works you did
Remain for us bereaving an exquisite array.
The joyful decades of friendship you and I embraced,
The tunes of sorrow my memory within me plays

And the tears and sighs my grieving heart compressed
Shall roam over my soul for my remaining days.

Gad's reflections on various issues exhibit the depth of his interest in and observation of social or political issues. Here's an excerpt of his poem "*Humanity, Unredeemed*" referring to human frailties and their consequences:

Adam and Eve the apple ate
And merrily leapt to procreate;
The Prophets since and godly kings
Built up virtue on the swings.

Poets followed, scientists and philosophers
Sketched the world and living in avid colours
While the serpents of hate and greed kept crawling
Mauling virtue, love and peace, ever mauling.

In his poem, "*The Uprising*", which Gad wrote following the so-called uprising in the Middle East and North Africa in 2011, he laments the ambitions of religious or political tyrants:

Against the blank of rights and law
they will not sing praises
or raise red and white roses.
The sound of fury run high and low.
Will pigeons and angels fill the space
Of pious words and naked want?
Or tiger snakes will creep in place
And hiss the venom with sugared font?

Away from his lamentations, Gad enjoyed turning to happier occasions such as the 69th birthday party of his wife Judith. Here's an extract from his poem "*Effervescent, Superfine*":

At the age of something-nine
You look as young as forty-nine,
Animating as red wine
Effervescent, superfine
May well be hailed as divine
Thank heavens you are mine.

And on her 70th Birthday party, Gad recited his poem *"Ode to Joujou" (Joujou* being the nickname he always used when calling her). Here's an extract:

We met by chance and warmly courted,
I felt her heart must no matter win
We danced and drank and keenly flirted
And felt the waves of Tonic and Gin.

My life with her is manna from heaven
When earth is calm and the sky bright;
My wishes are met sooner than given
On a sunny day or a moony night.

The poems of Gad Ben-Meir express deep emotions. He does not seek reserved expression. His vocabulary is rich, his style clear and unambiguous. The experience of love and the pain of separation or estrangement are dominant in many of his poems. He does not employ complicated metaphors, amazing images, masked allusions or intricate symbols.

Gad sings his heartbeats in his unequivocal poetic expression.

LOVE
POEMS

GLOWING RAPTURE

(A message from her heart)

Ennoble my feelings, call me Darling,
No sweeter melody I could hear;
The glittering rays of every morning
Enshrine it well in my ear
And arouse the yearnings of a bride
To thrust the hidden veils aside
And let the passion long encased
With yours to be fast embraced.

Ennoble my feelings, call me Darling
The word sparks a glowing rapture
And makes each day a new adventure.
My dreams with yours shall combine
And our souls gracefully entwine.
I'll wrap you with my shy desire
And embrace your caressing fire

Of that, my love, I'll never tire.

DANCING FANCIES

(Fighting the odds and gaining her new love)

Mother Eve, Moses, Ezra and Nehemiah[1],
Witness my weariness, the revealing marks
Of my descent from the stars of Utopia
To the puddles where my opponent barks,
Masking the truth behind false paraphernalia;
Ever ready to join the mutiny of sharks.

I am the daughter of Jerusalem,
Mother of my daughters of Zion.
As an oak tree I stand against him
In pride, trifling his ghastly frown.
Yes, I am bruised, hurt and thinned,
Yet steadfast, braving his sullen wind;
With Galahad's heart and cocktail drink
My spirit shall rise and his shall sink.

Not I shall remain grey
Nor let melancholy sway
The celestial lights caressing my fancy.
Convert I will to rhythmic odyssey
With all orchestral silences, restless discontent,
Worry, monotony and the void of lament.
'Cause a noble heart shall remain sublime
And a lowly hound ever a Pantomime.

Let the red wine of *Hebron,*[1]
Glow brightly in my cheeks
And the sunny sky of *Gideon*[2]
My dormant desire streaks.

And you, my new feverish throb,
Who came to enchant and rob
With your crimson lips
And your melodious quips
The bubbles of my swirling desire
And the spikes of my latent fire.

Behold your penetrating gaze,
Hold me with your poetic phrase;
I'll pluck from the garden of my heart
Roses and tulips to adorn the mast
Of your nourished gallant affection
And lubricated waltzing seduction.
Then roam in the meadows
Of my restless yearning
And breathe the fragrance
Of my passion burning.

No longer shall I miss my earthly pleasure,
For gaining a heavenly prize;
It's you I boldly wish to closely treasure,
And let the saints to heaven rise.

---

1   Two great Jewish reformers in Judea under the rule of the Persian Empire during the years 445-433 BCE.

2   Two settlements in Judea during the same period in (1) above, currently in the West Bank.

Come, sweet racer, rush to my post
You'll find my heart your clamouring host.
Let's traverse the valleys, the hills, the meadows
Of sweet Jerusalem and shed our sorrows,
Hear our hearts prattle, our passions sing
And our fancies dance to the tunes of spring.

THE POET AND THE PRINCESS

At home the noble, courageous Princess,
Restless with thoughts, yearnings to caress,
Daughter of pride and lofty manners,
Never proclaims her feelings on banners.

Out in the fields of her country's battle
Her sword is sharp, ready to scuttle
The evil designs against her Tribe
And blunt the tongues that rail and jibe.

No shrines of glory or wreaths of fame
The Princess aspires from victory to gain;
Only the land her people claim
And suffer no more or shudder in vain.

With the pause of the thunder
And the lull of the gust,
The Princess' thoughts began to wander
In the meadows of her lust.

She called the Poet with veiled refrain
And loud they laughed together again.
They chatted and dared and crashed the walls
Of crumpled norms and dreary calls.
And when she sent his heart to spin
Quick came the Poet her heart to win.

The Poet dreamt as full moon she shone,
Her passion high, a glamorous throne,

The flirt and longing in her glance
Revved up his soul to roam and dance.
She granted her cheeks but shied her lips
And deep she sparked her warmth in heaps.

The Poet faced her waves, her tide
And saw her lips honeyed with pride,
He thanked the fate that had them tied
Over the flame that neither shied.
They danced and danced as two butterflies
And rainbows they saw in each other's eyes.

The Poet gently said:

"May it please you to lie and rest
And let your fancies climb the crest?
Blossom you will with cheering pleasure
And make me feel I am your treasure."

And the Princess softly intoned:

"Close the shutters, dim the light,
Unfold my shackles and never tire.
Sip the wine and hold me tight,
And let my lips light the fire."

TROPHIES OF ADULATION

Mistress of my dreams, my beautiful flower,
No tyrant but your love over me has power,
So much yearning I have in me sustained,
To be by your touch blissfully ordained.

Wish I could in my heart enthrone you,
And feel with precious gems enriched,
Then heap all love trophies on you,
And remain, with your beauty bewitched.

Nothing along the ripening of age,
Can but romance assuage,
Come, distant darling, lay by my side
And let our desires sway and stride;
Swiftly by them we daringly abide
And love will rise to heaven deified.

Let's ride to new horizons far away,
All rounds, bounds and mountains we sway.
Your fountain shall, in my patient well,
Pour ravishing passion and joy to dwell.
In unison we doze, we dream, awake
And all life's barriers gently brake.

I Look and Dream and Wonder

I see your picture smiling in splendour,
In wordless song calling my name,
I look and dream and gaily wonder,
How can you not my heart inflame?

Yes, I am real, a nightingale of love,
Portrayed in your cradled yearning,
Real to sing to his distant dove,
The songs she craves of passion burning.

Not you shall I ever forget
Or lose my crowning hope,
Each dawn, each glowing sunset,
With your soul in joy elope.

YES, COME TO ME

You and I by fate are made
To each other a serenade,
The bounty of a glorious hour
Undaunted by terrestrial power.

When your laughter begins to ring
My heart shall merrily sing,
And when my whispers rouse your appetite
I know I've gained my heavenly delight.

Say I shall come to you, I shall
And leave to rot the ugly and dull,
Ruffle my hair, caress my head,
And let our souls happily wed.

Be you my sun, my moon, my star,
My joy will then fly up afar,
I'll write my name on your face,
And hail the grace of the human race.

We'll chase the Devil out of the clock
And crown the angel with a satin frock.
Our passion will light up like the rising sun,
And love will sing "*I am your only son*".

Our spirits shall float serene,
Above the cloud of narrow days,
Reflect, may be, on what has been,
And sip the joy in a thousand ways.

Come, sweet love, hurry and come,
I've blown the trumpet and beaten the drum.
Over the bed of roses our romance's tale
Will gladden the heart of the nightingale
Singing to us, up in the sky:
"Love is alive, caution must die."

SHEHERAZADE

Oh, I wish, how I wish
To usurp Cupid's wings,
Fly over your golden arches,
Perch on your laced chamber,
Chase away the nightingales,
And hug the serenade of your heart.

I'll embrace your desire,
Wear your fire,
And celebrate on the sunrise of love
The silence of Nirvana
As did lovers in Verona.

Be you my *Sheherazade,*
Beautiful, eloquent, charming, loving
And I, your *Thief of Baghdad*
Gallant, passionate, adoring.
Airborne on my Magic Carpet
I bring you the love I stole
From the hearts of all lovers
Wrapped with the rainbow of desires
And the rosy delights of
The Thousand and One Nights.

I'll crown you as the Princess of my universe,
Hug the seduction radiating from your eyes,
And together fly to the heights of
The Thousand and One Nights.

We'll then submerge,
As did lovers in Verona,
Into the silence of Nirvana.

THE EAGLE HAS LANDED

The eternal teenager of love,
Calls his beloved dove,
When her dreams climax at dawn,
And she rises to his throne.

He breathes her living flowers,
Cajoles her happy hours,
The dreary days vanish into the starry night,
And passions fray with wings of delight.

Her touch and scent and amorous sounds,
Arouse his passion beyond all bounds,
And change his wants and earthly fears,
To erotic yearnings she warmly cheers.

He gamely sucks her flickering fire,
And revels in her twinkling passion,
He tastes the wine of her desire,
And lights the candle of life's elation.

She mirrors his amorous smile,
Entwines with the touch she craves;
She flutters with his sails a while
And rides along his toxic waves.

They spill the salt water of strife,
And sip the sweet wine of life,
The eagle lands head on tail,
Their world becomes a nightingale.

THE BREEZE OF YOUR FRAGRANCE

He will cross the immortal seas
And see you
Hailing his arrival
To your naked shores
With radiant smile,
Heralding the first joyous kiss,
The fullness of life's bliss,
The passion
Of a new-born love.

He dreams,
Like a nightingale in mid-air
Swaying with
The breeze of your fragrance
And the rays of your beauty;
Glorying in new-found happiness
And the ravishing delight
Of togetherness on a sunny day
Or a starry night.

Let's forget, he says, the turbulent world,
Its pains, fears and woes;
Loosen our chains
And rejoice
On the flowery fields of love.
The spring of our feelings
Will tingle through our veins
And Our spirits and hopes
Rise above the plains.

He pampers himself with the hope
Of seeing you in the flesh
Riding the gondola of love,
Caressing your feelings
With the waves of his yearning
And tame your twirling desire
As you may crave to sail
Making transient life
A gift, a song, a fairy tale.

THE BEACH WALKER

I walk on the beach,
On an overcast morning,
I think of you, think of you,
Far into the horizon I stare,
I see you floating
At the end of the rainbow,
Naked,
As the mermaid
Is naked,
As the dolphin
Is naked,
As the faint sunrays
And the caressing breeze
Are naked.

Smiling, I see you,
Stretching your arms
Inviting me to ride the waves,
To usurp the eagle's wings,
Fly up and land on your rainbow.

I fly, I call your name and reach for you;
"*fear not*", I say, "*doubt not*" I intone,
"*The wind of passion is my rocket,
Incendiary yearnings dance in my veins,
And my love, untamed, as dictator, reigns*"

On your rainbow I see you
Running towards me,

Arms stretched,
Red and white roses in both hands and
A nightingale on each shoulder.

I run to you,
Embrace you fervently and
I wake up in my bed
Embracing my pillow instead.

HEART TO HEART SHALL RALLY

Lay your head on my chest,
Banish the restless thoughts
And whisper the loving ballads.
Heart to heart shall rally,
Body and soul shall nest
And joyfully reach the crest.
The stars will dance to your tune;
As will the shy smiling moon.

The melody of my yearning
Turns to jubilation,
The cravings I've nurtured
Your dalliance will embrace.
Let's eat, drink and romance
To Cupid's exultation.
The naked love we grace
No power can efface.

RENDEZ-VOUS IN THE SKY

As you shine in my crimson sky
The trumpets of welcome will blow at once;
The butterflies of joy will bloom and fly
And the birds in my heart merrily dance.

I'll breathe your fragrance
With the vagrant breeze
While the towers of
My patience tumble down;
I'll ask space and time
To quickly freeze
And Cupid to enthrone you
With lover's crown.

Yes, unload your dreams
On my fertile meadow
And reap the longing,
The hugging and the passion,
New dreams will surge
With poetic billow
And all pious thoughts
Shall abandon the prison.

I, the Redbreast, you the butterfly,
Shall roam together in the crimson sky,
Usurp the wings of time,
And live to love and rhyme.

LIFE AND LOVE

I bask with those who smile,
And shun all those who frown,
Cause life is only a while
And love its glorious crown.

Love never stays still,
Makes lovers rise uphill,
Bubbly and fresh
In spirit and flesh
As their souls inspire
And their hearts desire.
Becoming a serenade, a flare
Time shall not wantonly impair.

The book lovers open
At the dawn of their voyage,
Reveals the rainbow of their souls.
Its folded pages beam
The wonder and passion,
The dreams and delight
Of life's precious gift:
The marriage of two hearts.

Row leisurely, you lucky lovers,
Your hearts dancing, your passions singing
Where the sun shines and the moon smiles
And remain entranced for long, long whiles.

PARADISE GAINED

Ages since we talked my love,
When you wrapped your juicy words
With melodious voice
And flashed them across the seas
To my bumpy shores.
They caressed my yearning
Like a breeze,
Carrying the amorous butterflies
To their beloved roses
In the play fields.

The wonder of each day
More wondrous it shall be
With you,
Rowing my heart leisurely
With your gentle oars
To embrace your heart
In vibrant romance;
Our unsleeping passion
Our enchanting desires
Ruling the waves.

I'll lock you up
In my fantasy and
Shut off the world,
Dance to the ripples of your excitement,
Breathe the scent of your rapture,
Kiss your dewy, impatient lips,
And lift the lover's torch

In a triumphant march
To happiness
In Paradise gained.

ANOTHER MOMENT

From the Seine, to Pigalle to Eiffel Tower
Hand in hand they stroll and ascend,
With the breeze of the Seine
And the passion of Pigalle
And the music of La Fontaine
To the heights of the wonder
And the joy and splendour
Of life's worthiest gift:
The rowing of two hearts
In the Gondola of Love.

High above the lofty Tower
They live the magic and glamour
Their eyes reflect,
Their whispers convey,
And their hearts' throbs intone
While their kisses betray
The mystery of their souls
And the beauty of their goal.

At the top of the Tower
They sing with the birds above
The serenade of life in love.

Waiting for the Nightingale to Sing

(Patience deserted her)

The Stars dwindled,
The moon gone west,
Sunrise beckoned
And no hello to cheer the breast.

I wait for the nightingale to sing,
For the dove to bring the news;
The breeze and the waves swing
And silence sings the blues.

Patience does not obey
A loving heart pulsating,
Say whatever you may,
I am on fire waiting!

FIRST ENCOUNTER

The first was a meeting of strangers
Where the sun in another sky shone
And the meadows hosted lovers unknown;
A fragment of a dream conceived wonders.

The shadowy attraction gave birth
To breezes of thoughts streaming,
With words and voices beaming
The fragrance of engagement and mirth.

Gently they rowed the boat of years past,
And softly berthed on the shores of the future,
Where hopes and fears are a dormant feature
Of poets' souls in velvet cast.

Each took up high, flying contented,
Musing on what destination evokes,
With a mystery created in two strokes
And the vibes of love in wonder suspended.

The strangers soon became soul mates,
As if fate so decreed,
Nothing but love knows how to speed
A smitten heart to lover's gates.

THE SHADOW HAS GONE

The shadow has gone, sunshine beckoned
The morning coffee and the call of heart;
The breeze conveyed her romantic errand
To him who dwelt oceans apart.

They talked and laughed and soon forgot
The narrow days of solitude and pain;
The silent desire twinkled afloat
The bed of roses their dreams sustain.

Their hearts gladdened in festive glee
And felt elated, body and soul;
Life's blessings are best when free
From weathered limbs or failing calls.

HEART SHALL NOT DISPENSE
WITH HEART
(with a shattered hope he wrote to her)

I see you wrapped in fur and glow,
Glamour to the trees, the birds, the snow,
Eyes, with daring looks flirting,
Smile, a rendezvous inviting.

You know so well, a few days ago
My hopes ran high in vertigo,
Yearning to sip from your lips
The honey of love and amorous quips;
But fate said no and shattered all hopes
Drifting them down the dreary slopes.

Your love shall always cheer mine,
Illuminate my heart and shape my dream,
Elevate my soul where Angels shine
And make our hope in happiness stream.

Remain we may for a while apart,
But heart shall not dispense with heart,
By love's wings we shall roam the sky
And let our passion briskly fly.

Laughing, Loving, Loved in Heaps
(Missing her lover)

Come lay your heart on my breast,
And let my passion reach the crest,
My soul shall reach heaven on earth
Your love will be my life's worth.

I see you radiant with mirth and zest
And wish you always adorn my nest
Laughing, loving and loved in heaps
Lips on eyes and eyes on lips
Heart to heart with silent words
Tell the tales of nesting birds.

Come nurse my longing in fond embrace,
Drown the thorns of life and grace
Our love with caressing prose
And breathe the passion in my red rose.

THE LADY IN PINK PYJAMAS

She reclines alone on her deck chair,
Sipping her morning coffee in fresh air,
Rejoicing with the breeze kissing the birds,
Listening to the absent lover of melodic words,
With whom she longs to traverse the meadows
Of unshuttered thoughts and romantic billows

While the guardian is fast asleep.

Caressing hopes swirl her furtive mind,
With yearning for ecstasy combined,
Long she fought to guard the tree of life,
And cast away the eagles of strife.
Now it's time for loving and delight
Sunset may shine victory to her sight

And the eagles fall in a gloomy heap.

Quickly she calls her lover of rhyme
And says *Hello* in morning prime.
He breathed the scent of her lips in glee
And felt she longed for him to be
With her, embraced on a deckchair for two
Wearing pyjamas in deep sea blue

The colours merge and the two hearts leap.

THE MYSTERY TRAVELLER

Beautiful as a dove,
Roaming the sky of love,
She enters his world,
Romantically unfurled,
As a mystery traveller,
A tutored reveller,
To uncover his yearning
With desires swirling

In eloquent silence.

Watched by the moon and stars bright
In the floating hours of the night;
Her passion impatiently swells,
And the cupids ring a thousand bells.
At sunrise they prize the glaring marks
And hail the mysteries their nature sparks.
Serenity adorns their naked souls
And love within their hearts strolls

With triumphal resonance.

CARRY ME TO SUNLIGHT

(Hailing her new lover)

Come, dear beloved,
Illuminate my night,
With your shining eyes
And your fragrant rosy lips;
Make the hours a serenade
And the twinkling stars a parade,

No more sorrowing.

Arise, dear beloved,
Shine your love on my soul,
Uproot the treacherous dagger
Swung into my heart
By the hyena dressed as a deer
In a misty veneer,

Leaving my faith shivering.

Come, dear beloved
Carry me to sunlight
On the wings of your heart
Freed from my dreary plight.
I will dance to the magic tune
Of the reshining smiling moon

With my passion whispering.

When you reach me, sweet beloved
The waves, the lilies and the birds

Will hail your exotic dancing and
The buds of happiness bloom;
You will in my heart happily dwell
And your love shall be my life's cell

With all our stars glittering.

BLESSED SOULS

I see your picture smiling in splendour,
In speechless song calling my name,
I look and dream and hope and wonder,
How can you not my heart inflame?

Yes, I am real, a nightingale of love,
Only imagined in your cradled yearning;
Real to sing to his far away dove,
The thrilling songs of passion burning.

Not you shall I ever forget,
Or lose my patient hope,
Each dawn, each crimson sunset,
I shall with you elope.

HE WISHED, HE WISHED

She has smiles to charm the eye
Of all beings on earth and sky,
To win her heart one needs a spark,
Of heavenly traits and magical mark.

Fresh as a rose she looks, as a princess she talks,
Like the breeze of spring she moves and walks.
Sweet is her laughter, sweeter her touch,
Awake or dreaming, he misses her so much.

In her melodious voice he felt
The swing of his desire,
Like a spring of love in him she dwelt;
And he wallowed in her fire.

She dropped her anchor by his heart
And swam through his throbbing veins,
Never shall he from her depart,
Or cast away her loving chains.

Imagine then his pride and joy
When she asked to give her a hoy,
She uprooted his heart in one refrain
He wished, he wished she asks again.

I RUSH TO CALL ON FATE

I listen to your heart
Whispering my name;
I read in your thoughts
The verse of wonderment;
I hear in your voice
The waterfalls of emotion;
I see in your eyes
The rays of nestling love
And, in your feathered nest
I sing with
Your melodious passion.

I rush to call on fate
To abandon its patience
And set the course
For a wondrous horizon
Where our eager souls
Become a poem
And our silent desires
A roaring duet.

THE PERFUMED TEMPLE OF LOVE

On a moon spiced night,
Out of my feverish imaginings,
Rose this poem to greet you
Whilst you are sipping
Your morning coffee and
Ruminating over the surreal melody
Of a trance with your absent lover
Weaving through your veins.

Not the one whose flourish is drying
And whose feelings sighing.

No, the one who cruises through
Your aromatic thoughts and
Glides over your sparkling passion.

There, on the hills, under full moon,
You sweep away
The distracting tensions,
The stressful memories
And erect with him
The perfumed temple of love.

There, your souls will fervently entwine
And the moon smile to your enticing signs.

SILENT MELODIES

The silent moments
When your virgin image
Meander over my dreaming heart
To the tender tunes of
Mendelssohn's melodious classics
I convert his *Midsummer Night's Dream*
Into a vivacious Tango
With you;
We gallop over the stars
With incandescent desires
And clamorous lips.

You and I, the leading dancers,
Will give all Mendelssohn admirers
And all princes and princesses of love
The joy of life and
Hear them all applaud
Our adorable serenade.

Those heavenly moments of ecstasy
Will greatly outshine eternity.

A LONG, SILENT KISS

Exchanging silent cravings and
Extending anxious arms
Across the oceans.
With the birds, the dolphins
And the spring breeze
Our audience,
We give each other
A big hug and feel
The will of one
Embracing the will of the other
With exuberant eloquence
Brushing away the ghosts of reason
And life's humming disappointments.

Just for a few moments
We reap the prize
Of relished delight
And jump with it, naked
Into the pool of intimacy
Where illusions mock reality
And feelings rule over the waves.

Before we say goodbye
Across the oceans
We give each other
A long, silent kiss.

THE ROAD TO YOU IS LONG

The road to you is long,
With rocks and slopes abound,
But the tree of love is strong
And hope is curling around.

What joy can you feel all alone,
In a weaned, dreaming gilded bed?
While ghosts of hounds hanging on
Fake morals with evil eyes they spread.

Forsake all pains, all anger and lament
As wild thorns they grow and grow;
The birds shall then sing to your hearts' content
And tears of love, joy and bliss bestow.

Get up and rush and light the candle
And let its rays flush your passion,
Our souls shall glow and all malice throttle
And the sighs of love rhyme in slow motion.

The road to you is long
With rocks and slopes abound
But the tree of love is strong
With branches curling around.

WILL RING YOU SOON

Will ring you soon, she said, *will ring you soon*,
The flowers will smile facing the moon,
Her sonnet of love for so long silent,
Eclipsed by sad lament of the wicked tyrant.

He waits and waits and fervently hope,
Her pains and sorrows without a trace elope;
Lilies and roses will greet her shining face
And her carols of love his embrace.

He cannot imagine greater delight
Than cajoling her on a starry night;
Her nascent love revealing untapped pleasures
While Cupid keeps waving his magic treasures.

Will ring you soon, she said, *will ring you soon*,
my passion is booming facing the moon

TIME AND SPACE

Time and space, woes or pain breed not despair
To loving hearts that patience and hope inspire;
Sweet memories of happy days arm them to bear
Whatever ebbs the flow of what they most desire.

Alas, she feels lonely and bored
Yet her voice sparkles colourful tunes
Of satiable passion long while stored
Awaiting her erotic wings to flutter soon.

Yes, passions aren't easy to place on hold
When memories of loving are keen and bold;
Her lover will chant her fluffy dreams
And joyfully hail her intimate beams.

TWO HEARTS ENTWINED

Our paths must have crossed
When we were young,
Two hearts entwined, now
As then, with fancy strung.
No, not this fancy has
Been or soon be sated;
Not until Cupid's wings
With Venus' honey
are saturated.

Venus will then
Stroll in the vine
The new delights sailing
Through her dreaming breast;
Her smiles of joy and
Her crimson lips look divine
With revelling wishes,
Daring passion
And amorous zest.

YOU CHARM THE STARS WITH RHYME

You charm the stars
With soothing rhyme
And kiss the moon
With juicy winks;
Your yearnings quiver
And swirl on time
Voiceless, yet cleave
The crouching Sphinx.

In the distant horizon
Your face is shining
Violets and lilies
You flower and kiss;
The thorns of life
No longer prowling
And the labial flame
Shall cuddle the bliss.

Let's walk on the beach
And sketch on the sand
The rhythm of our hearts
And a soft emotive song,
Then sail with the flow
To the long-promised land
And cherish the desires
We have nursed for so long.

THE MAIDEN FAIR

Behold, the Maiden Fair
Has raised the mast
And steered the Gondola
With sails of passion.
She berthed in triumph
With her Lover
Where no qualms or shadows
Dare to hover
Nor the sweet roses
Of joy ever wither.
The tunes of love
Were from heaven cast.

They softly sank
In their rosy dreams
While the dolphins played
The primordial game.
She struck the gong
With tulips and peonies
And set him aflame
With sensuous melodies.
The swinging birds
Sang their parodies
And sunrise beamed
Its prodigious seams.

As a newly bloomed flower
The Maiden Fair smiled and sighed
And her handsome gallant Lover
Breathed her enticing repose;

Her fadeless fragrance ravished the air,
His soul, his heart, his mind, his flair.

Amorous she whispered:
"I am your Maiden Fair"
And he lovingly quipped:
"and I am your loving pair".

RESUMED THEIR SEARCH
FOR THE KEYS

Yes, she shone on the sands
With an eye for romance
And she saw him
Amply fitting her desires;
She feigned losing car keys
To attract his advance
And he rushed to
The treasure he aspires.

Her sirens beckoned her desire
All his passion quickly fire.
She called him *Lovey*
And intoned with flair:
Are you ready for a stunt
Where the guard has never been?
Fast he quipped:
"Your will, my command, all you dare."

She is sexy, bold and bubbly,
Magic prize from the sky
Just the Darling his roving soul
Bravely craves.
With Eros' halo shining
In her fiery sea blue eye
They galloped and dived
Where passions rule the waves.

Lovey ploughed all her meadows
And caressed her quest,

46

While the fairies
Gaily danced on the trees;
They sang with glee
Their romance on the crest
Then resumed
Their search for the keys.

ODE TO HER GALLANT LOVER

Hold me with your poetic phrase,
Caress me with your amorous gaze,
Let me pluck from the garden of my heart
A thousand flowers and make you a tart
To intoxicate your waltzing affection
And nourish your gallant seduction.

Then roam in the meadows
Of my restless yearning
And breathe the fragrance
Of my passion burning.

EROS' KEY

The ship of life
Not always plainly sails,
Nor does it always
Reach its port;

But when the breeze
Of moonlit sea prevails
And the lovers land
On the far resort

All cares are dumped
And life garlands worn.
Eros' key will shine
And all veils swiftly torn.

ANGELS ENVY HER
SWEET SURRENDER

The Bard is there watching the stars,
Hoping to see his Venus beaming;
'Cause once her rays touch his spars
Nothing will bar his passion daring.

Nothing can Venus then withhold;
Certainly not her amorous splendour.
And when the inner rhymes turn bold
The Angels envy her sweet surrender.

CUPID'S TRIUMPH

You have touched the meadow
Where my love's roses grow
And the strings of untamed heart
Play the tunes of blood aglow.
Shame the wide, wild chaining oceans
Keep our fertile passions apart.

I float on the rocking waves facing
The snow-white roving clouds, feeling
The Magic of your fingertips,
Dreaming of you face to face smiling
While the sonorous breeze absorbs
The silence of our quivering lips.

Our souls will then hum in unison
The sonata of amorous elation,
Inhale the fragrance of flaming kisses
And gulp the juice of scintillating passion.
Smiling Cupid will perch on our ivory towers
And hail his triumph over our senses.

ROVING INTO THE WINGLESS NIGHT

The sails are frail and the wind angry
And the groans are drumming the blues,
Yet his heart and his soul are hungry
For stranded passions to cruise.

Lo and behold, her voice arose
Scattering the bleak twigs of gloom;
Her night dress and white rose
Heralding their dreams to bloom.

They go intensely roving
Late into the wingless night;
Their hearts surging, roaring
Their passion shining bright.

Love remains their souls' red wine
And ecstasy its soaked red wings,
Nothing more ravishing or divine
Or akin to the bliss it springs.

Yes, it can also harshly enslave
All tides, all thoughts, all wiles
And fears and desolation engrave
On the rocks of bereaved smiles.

But he sees her emitting loving rays
While the smiling moon winks in jest
Watching their swinging forays
Into the dazzling, luscious crest.

THE TREE OF HOPE

Run, run past your shadow
Usurp the Angel's wings
Fly, fly to my world
And, when you see
My heart pierced with silent woes
And my lips tied with patience,
You know I have abandoned all masks,
All noxious memories,
And stood up like a tower of hope
Waiting for you to invade my heart,
Waving the banner of love
And the wreath of intimacy.

You guide me with your eyes
To your dancing heart;
I hug you and whisper
With inflamed tones:

*You are the queen of my world
And the ruler of my desires
And I want you.*

The Mazurka of time will resume
And we both sing:

*We steer our hearts towards the sun
And feel our passion alight
And when we reach the crest as one
We shine amorous delight.*

WALTZING WITH YOU

Let your gentle fingers
Through my hair
And your whispers
Cajole my ears;
Flesh on flesh,
Soul with soul,
Love shall wear
The shroud of fire
And dress our wants
With ravishing attire.
We'll recite melodiously
The poetry of night
And dance the waltz
Of our ravishing delight.

Life shall then by joy,
Not sorrow, nursed
And long desired love,
By inspiration versed
Unfolding the magic
Of uncharted mysteries
And chanting our desires
With novel melodies.

I see your eyes shining, beaming;
I see your lips as red roses blooming;
I see your cheeks with passion glowing
And I your desires rowing, rowing.

WHERE UNTAMED WISHES STRAY

I see you in my dream standing
On the swirling waters of the beach;
The breeze waving your crimson hair and
Your smile revealing the love in your heart.
Your blue swim suit uncovers
The rays of your seduction and
The sparkles of untamed wishes.

I look at you, look at you,
Imagine your fervent passion
Whirling in your veins
And feel my tortured desire
Vanishing with you under the silvery waves
And rolling into the meadows of Eden
Where the embers of love glow and glow.

I feel we are misplaced in time,
Graced by the perfume
Of your poetic radiance,
Oscillating between dreams and reality.
We ride the waves of love
In the ocean of yearning souls.

I look at you, I see you laughing
And all seasons turn to spring;
The roses blossom to greet your smile and
The birds dance to the resonance
of your laughter.
I hug you and kiss you
Dreaming in isolation.
Hope becomes a prized consolation.

THE TOUCH AND THE TASTE

The Touch and the Taste
In the Eden of Love
Trump the serpent
And the apple and the curse;
When the vortex of passion
Swirl through the veins
The angels sing
The erogenous verse
And we rise up high
To the jubilant crest
Where our hearts
The winged delights nurse.

KINDRED REFLECTIONS

Sailing through
The ravishing waves,
Hugging the memories
My heart craves
Reaching the shores
Of amorous dreams.
That's when the moon
Smilingly beams
Seeing us hugging
The silence of time
And the loving exchange
Of tuneful rhyme.

Rise up and hail
The birds to sing
And dance to
Every tune you fancy;
We'll embrace
The fragrance of spring
And bury strife
In the deep blue sea.

I DREAM SEEING YOU FLYING

I dream seeing you flying
In the fragrant gardens of heaven,
Adorned with wings of roses,
Amorous eyes twinkling,
Emitting rays of desire,
Igniting my dormant passion and
The fire of torrid consummation.

I see you shedding the roses,
Landing gently on my dancing heart,
Your cherry moist lips
With mine bravely entwined.
Thunder mad with delight
We float on Eros' gondola
And sail to the smiling horizon.

Pity it was all a day dream;
The roaring whirls of passion
Soon reversed, depressed
By the cold wind of plighted emotion
Coursing through the bloodstream.

I'll wait for the wind
to sway your sails to my shore
And for your sun to light the fire;
'Cause our souls are as one enshrined
And my hope shall never tire.

SWEET WILD DAUGHTER
OF JERUSALEM

I heard your voice gently intoning
Unspoken, entrancing fervent desire;
I felt our passions boldly entwining
To burn our days with amorous fire.
The smiling romance will wrap us shining
And the shimmering joy new sparks inspire.

I hold you in my heart and shut the world
With all its woes, hatreds and deeds unfair;
The ripples of your heart will sing the word
And swell my yearning with erotic flare.
The angel of love and the singing bird
Will nourish our souls with amorous flair.

You defy the odds and challenge fate
And sail through life with ferric wisdom;
With playmate's voice and disarming haste
Your soul flourish and your wants blossom.
Pray blow the siren and mount the crest,
Sweet wild daughter of Jerusalem.

CALLING YOUR NAME

I walk and dream and cajole the breeze
And see in the rainbow your smiling face;
I watch the seagulls over the seas
And wish I could fly and your heart embrace.

I lay on the beach in quiet retreat
And listen to my heart calling your name;
My naughty thoughts silently entreat
Your passion to rise and mine tame.

The love you have poetically unlaced
With your captivating melodious tongue
And the charm you have modestly embraced
Will live and flourish delectably young.

Let's steer our hope towards the sun,
And feel our vibrant veins alight;
And when we meet and breathe as one
We'll shine through the moonlit night.

Yes, it all remains a wondrous dream
The nascent dawn dares not repress;
Our whirling passion will glow and beam
With fragrant wonder all lovers impress.

In the Deep of the Night

You shone and flushed
My heart with joy
And set the bells
Of love ringing;
The hours of life
Are meant to enjoy
Leaving the drums
Of worries banging.

Silence may speak
A thousand words
Not after
Those encoded;
The angels above
My heart heard
With no cooling
Throbs invested.

I heard your voice
Gently intoning
Unspoken, entrancing
Sweet desire;
I felt our passions
Boldly entwining
To flood our veins
With amorous fire;
The melodious sighs
Will wrap us shining
And the shimmering joy
New sparks inspire.

RHAPSODIC DELIGHTS

Those were incandescent moments
Refusing to dissolve
Into the mist of yearning and
Float away with memory.

He fervently wished them
To be with her
In a secret garden,
Ready to hear
Vignettes of her verse
And see her blossom
With orchidaceous passion.

There he tastes her sugary smile,
Touch her vibrating lips,
Wallow in her seductive eyes,
And feel the ripples
Of their swollen hearts
Humming the tunes
Of unlocked desires.

There, in the silence
Of moonlit nights
They navigate
Their rhapsodic delights.

THE ROAD DIDN'T END THERE

He stood by the gate of hope,
Trees in the park dancing
Birds singing.
Like a rippling summer breeze
She flowed towards him
Fresh, vibrant, majestic
Flushed with erotic brilliance;
The Empress of love and seduction
With mighty shadowless will
Outshining the sun.

With taming looks
And intimate grip
She held his arm and led him
To embark on the journey
To the treasures in her meadows
And the rainbows in her inner world.
No greater joy he had ever felt
Than being detained
By such an adorable tyrant.

Swamped with longing
And bloated with passion
The trip flourished with unveiled romance.
Words were lost in her honey dewed lips
And his caressing tongue;
Entranced with hugging and kissing
Time disappeared.
Onlookers sat silent, honouring

Their virgin mesmeric union
With Cupid sailing in their veins.

Merry, radiating abundance
Of colourful temptation
They entered her paradise;
The birds playfully witnessed
The union of their inflamed desires
And the muffled flow of ecstasy.
Those rhapsodic moments
Dissolved into
The scent of haunted flesh
And floated around
With their drunken hearts.

The semen of chance
Encounter years before
Flourished into a wreath
Of conjugal flowers
Diffusing the fragrance
Of incandescent love.

Dazed by the new born fortune,
Their rejuvenated souls
Embarked on the waves
Of her poetic treasures
Listening to his ethereal voice
Reciting their touching evocations.

Tears of intimacy
Roved gently in her eyes.

He felt his voice
Resonating in her blood
And her roaming tears
Penetrating his heart.
Her inspiring verse
Moved them like dancers
To music played in heaven.

The new champions of love
Conquered the odds
And unsealed its mystery.
In that short heavenly bliss
The clamour of their souls
And the howling of their passion
Crossed the threshold of time
And rolled their naked bodies
Into Adam and Eve's paradise
To relish the taste
Of ripened apples!

He came back to the world;
He walked on the beach
On a wintery day.
The footsteps of man and dog
Defied the weather.
On the far-flung horizon
He saw the sky
Embracing the sea
And the memory
Of the dream he lived
Recapture his vision

And rekindle
His desire, his hope, his will
To feel her intimate grip
Leading him, again, to her meadow
To reunite with her quixotic soul
And the tides of her love,
His fair Creole Lady.

The first journey was over
But the road didn't end there.
Butterflies will keep
Adorning the meadows
And the nightingales
Merrily sing.

BUT HEED IT WILL

Oceans are deep,
Mountains are high,
But love is deeper
And flies higher;
Streams through the senses,
brighten the views
And sings the tunes
Of toxic desires.

Fondly cherished,
Always adored,
Pardons the lover
When wearing a shroud;
But heed it will
When sanguinely implored
Fluttering its wings
And bursts the cloud.

SWOONED FOR JOY

He thought of you and no time left
For day or night dreaming;
He locked you in his sodden heart
And felt your love streaming.

Your daring breast and juicy tongue
With hungry lips he cherished
And saw you bloom, swooned for joy
And all his woes soon perished.

THE DREAM OF THE POEM

Rise up, rise up and face the sun
And tell the birds *I am the one*
Who sings the songs of love and run
With him who braved my heart and won.

Reclining, blooming, shading the moon
Awaiting his call, her distant lover;
With starving passion and ravishing tune
She plunges with him into the naked river.

For each other, heart and soul
They expose their love across the oceans;
They rise and yield to Cupid's call
And thank their fate for stormy passions.

EMBALMED IN YOUR FRAGRANCE

Embalmed in the fragrance of your beauty
And the lyricism of your verse
He awaits your return to his nest
Where your lips are honey to his
And your looks a rainbow to his eyes.

At day-break he imagines you stretching
Over the lonesome couch of dreams
Echoing the soundless pearls of love.
Soon the Nightingale merrily flutters
And chants the song of Cupid's return.

THE BLUE NIGHTY

He sends you wreaths of heavenly flowers
And invites you to wander
In the meadows of romance
Where a glance reveals the naked desire
And a whisper plays the dancing fire.

He sails on your blue nighty's tides,
Uncover your soul and beating heart
And feels your love's ardent eyes
Flashing emotional outpourings
On the dawns of erotic mornings.

SHE OPENS HER SPLENDOURS

Sweet Darling lay alone
In her yearning nest
When her lover calls
At the break of day;
Her glowing hello
swells his romantic zest
And swiftly slides
Into her beauteous bay.

Her vanities rise up
With his winning kiss
And the daring desires
Ride the tide;
She opens her splendours
And hail the bliss
And the birds sing along
The vigorous ride.

Sweet Darling wakes up
In her blue nightgown
Caressed with the fragrance
Of the hydrangeas;
Her lover flew away
Wearing Cupid's crown
Destined to whirl
In the vortex of her eyes.

ENTRANCED I LIE

The pulse of her fingers
Slowly stroking my silent limbs
Stirs the whisper of air
Inspiring sweet, serene delight.

Her long lithe arms,
With palms smoother than silk
Meandering with
The tunes of soft music,
Tenderly caressing my back
South to north, north to south
In vibrant, soothing succession.
Not a word, not a whisper
Invade the sweet thoughts
Caressing my dreaming head
And the serenity of
Blissful pleasure.

Entranced I lie
In happy submission
Until the hour flies away
Like a butterfly in a dream
Leaving a feeling of triumph
Over the hustle and bustle of the day.

A master act by Simone[3]
A magic treat, all her own.

---

3 *A Remedial Massagist*

LILIES AND ROSES GREET YOUR FACE

(consoling him and lifting his spirit for the pains he suffered)

I yearn and yearn and fervently hope
Your pains and lament roll down the slope;
Lilies and roses will adorn your face
And your carols of love mine embrace.

Cannot imagine a greater delight
Than being with you on a starry night
Your love revealing untapped pleasures
And Angels hailing your precious treasures.

Vividly, you cross the rapid
Swarming waves of desire
And hail the splendour of Cupid
Feeding roses to your fire.

A sound of passion deep in your heart
Ringing aloud, nourished to sprout
And send the birds skyward free
Merrily flying over the sea.

Sweets and wine host your space
Wit and laughter adorn your grace;
A passionate heart a crown you wear
With undaunted will all barriers tear.

Will ring you soon, will ring you soon
When your desire blooms facing the moon;
Your tunes of love for a while silent
Will capture my heart like a warring tyrant.

HER LOVE IS AGELESS

Up from heaven that glorious day was cast
Never so arousing, never so sweet;
Fragrant with passion marched boldly fast
To crush all shackles when eye to eye meet

She dreamt their lips sank into a fevered kiss
And all distance swiftly shrank to naught;
Dazzled by the dawn of the heavenly bliss
Her soul danced on Eros' waves afloat.

Love may fade upon the edge of time;
Hers is ageless, conceived by fate divine
Nourished by tender loving sublime
She silently sings *you are always mine.*

Not vexed by matter or marred by guilt
Their hearts married across cyberspace
And hoped in tandem a castle built
To crown them as lovers from outer space.

Lost in Your Wistful Eyes

He heard your voice,
Your loving parting words
Leaping over the mountains
Across the oceans
Enthralling his heart and
Decorating his soul
With the flowers of her passion.

She went away
Galloping from sun to moon
Leaving him kindled
By her silent kiss,
Seeking solace
In his imagination:
The mirror
Of her seduction.

He looked into her eyes and,
Like a lightning bolt,
He found himself roaming in
The meadows
Of her heart
Tattooed with her
Bold amorous pattern
And caressed by the fragrance
Of her soul.

Like a caged bird
he sang the tunes
Of vagrant moods

And daring hope that soon
He and she
Turn as one, aflame.

That was the end
Of the beginning.
Night followed.
He saw the coloured lightning
Radiating from her eyes.
He heard her enchanting laughter
Echoing the birds of Paradise.

He glided fast
Into her tryst
In mean attire;
He waltzed around
Her masked desire
And hailed the sparks
Of her loving fire.

In sweet seclusion until sunrise
She was lost in his wistful eyes.

BREATHE THE SCENT
OF YOUR PASSION

I cannot fathom
The wonder of creation
Nor the presence
Of an Almighty God;
But I love the winking pigeon,
The smiling moon,
The cheerful spring,
The intimate winter sun,
The caressing sea waves.

Most of all,
As a singing nightingale
I love to perch
On your amorous nest,
Bid farewell
To all rocks and thorns,
Breathe the scent of your passion,
The melodies of your love, and
Read in your soul
The poem of love
Beautifully rhymed
And live the wonder of life
With you enshrined.

You'll soon desert
My intimate universe
A month of nights you sleep,
A month of mornings you wake up

Far away
From my obsession;
Yet, I feel
Locked unto you,
Yearning to be your nurse
To treat you
With my ravishing touch,
To celebrate
The oblivion of your pain
And saturate you
With the elixir of desire
With my wings
Folded around you
And your wings
Flapping with joy.

As the humming birds of a feather
We'll merrily flock together
When next I hear
Your entrancing hello
Intonating the song
Of love, light,
And life.

You Lay Awake

You lay awake quivering,
Ravaged by deafening silence.
What does the future hold
For your galloping years?
Continue wallowing
In the elixir of hope
Yearning?
Praying?
Or start climbing the heights
Of a new romantic marvel,
Sniffing rejuvenating ecstasy?

There, on the fresh heights of romance,
The days become wondrous dreams
And the nights a theatre of erotic fusion.
There
He will be waiting;
There
You will float on each other's soul
And swim in each other's fancy.

Time will fly away
With colourful wings.

HOLD MY SOUL WITH EAGER ARMS

She has jumped many hurdles
And will soon reach the crest
Where her heart throbs with rhyme
And her passion sings the tune.
She floats serene, flushes the sky
With twinkling charming zest
And reap the joy of loving
Facing the shining moon.

Hold my soul with eager arms,
She asks her lover,
and let me breathe
The scent you spread;
My heart elopes
To your charms
Merrily humming
Your serenade.

He reads in her eyes
The swelling desire
And she smiles to him
With randy lips;
Enchanted they plunge
Into the marvel fire
And crown their love
With singing tulips.

IF I HAD BALTHAZAR'S POWER

If I had Balthazar's power
To be anywhere by a thought,
Move people with my mind and
Travel in time;
I would in a flash
Perch on your nest,
Before midnight, knowing
You had cajoled your thirst
With a glass of red wine
Feeling Cupid's romantic shine.

I embrace you with my wings
And land on lover's island
In the Tigris River
Where our desires tango,
You unveil your passion
And invade mine
With randy looks.

There I surge into you,
Breathe the fragrance
Of your desire,
Slake my thirst
With your sweet lips
And feel the jubilance
Of your heart.

Gladness will shine in your eyes,
And your sighs splash delight

Over the twilight sky and
The serene waters of the Tigris.

You will then fly with me in time,
And choose the destination.
I ruffle my wings
And vest you in my heart.

If only, if only
I had Balthazar's power!

MY HOPE TO SEE HER FLOURISHED

My Hope to see her flourished
Like a rose in mid spring;
She flushed my heart with joy
Splashing a radiant chance
From her bedroom.
Together we see
The waves clucking
The silent rocks
Far away
In the distant shores.

I breathed the perfume
In her words,
The intoxication
In her mood and
The fluttering
of her sighs.

I flew high
Hugging her passion
With amorous wings
And freed our desire
Of all grey strings.

SWEET JOAN OF ARC

I heard your voice gently intoning
Unspoken, entrancing fervent desire;
I felt our passions boldly entwining
To burn our days with amorous fire.
The smiling romance happily shining

And the shimmering joy
New sparks inspire.

You bravely defy the odds, you challenge fate
And sail through life with purpose and wisdom;
You well nurse disarming haste
And see your aims like roses blossom.
Blow the siren and mount the crest

Sweet Joan of Arc,
Daughter of Jerusalem.

I'll hold you in my heart and shut the world
With its thorns, thistles and acts unfair;
Your heart's ripples around mine curled
Swell our yearning with erotic flare.
The Angel of love and romancing birds

Will nourish our souls
With amorous flair.

LOVING HEART ACHINGLY BREAKS

Praise her love waking up
After grey seasons
Of hibernation
In the starry silence
Of the nights
And the rattle and flap

Of the days
when frowning boredom strays.

Praise her love waking up
Diffusing the fragrance
Of reborn passion,
Radiating the lure
Of sparkling desire,
Unlacing the veils
Of harmonious chime

And flushing the fountain
Of romantic rhyme.

Praise her love evermore
Now, alas, sorely eclipsed
By shadows of sorrow,
Strain and stress
She deeply suffers
For her dear ones' sake.

It is the loving heart
That achingly breaks.

Not he or she should say goodbye
And shrink into silent seclusion
Forsaking the titillations
Of pleasure and fun,
The thunder of
Ravenous engagement

And the lure of
Ravishing contentment.

The thickening clouds do not prevail
Nor does the agony
Of living in the shadows;
The shrill of the heart
No woes can for long silence.
The souls flourish
With the whizzing spark

Of the lover's rays
Twinkling in the dark.

She will bravely defy the odds,
Fly through
The thorns and thistles and
Perch on her
Fluffy love nest.
With her wisdom,
flair and patience
Her smiles shall
Like roses blossom.

And to her sweet prince joyfully sings
A bird never tires of having wings

COME WITH THE WIND
(Addressing her beloved)

Come with the wind Sweet Prince,
Burst into my feathered nest,
Pour your romantic verse on my heart
And give my patience a new dream.

Steal you I will from your solitary nest,
Graft you on my tipsy desire,
Taste the aroma of your flushed skin
And feast on your erotic devotion;
With Orpheus humming
We hail the alluring crescendo.

In my arresting day dream
You light a candle;
We sip the red wine
and smile with our hearts
At the shining rhymes
Of your poetic vision.

The spears of longing will soon
Return to spike my voluptuous bent.
Rip I will your tempting recline
And whisper to you,
My flesh-lambent Prince,
A taunting Hallelujah
For love's contagious flame.

ALL RICHES IN VAIN

(Her new love trumps the pains she suffered)

No parting word shall I hear
From you or else I disappear;
Let's make merry, eat and drink
And let all sorrows deeply sink.

My wealth is vast
So was my pain,
When the dust is cast
All riches in vain
Aiming high at last
Grasping life again.

Your fragrant breaths
Life to me they shine;
Hold me and whisper
you are mine
Loving you then
Becomes a shrine.

Siren of the Heart

I'VE SANG MY SONG

I've sang my song and jumped the fence
And lost no time to plant the seeds;
I waited long for recompense
And got no more than shimmering weeds.

How far are you? Come back and let
Me blast the chill of dormant passion
A fond embrace of your breast
And one long kiss will fire elation.

Let not the music of love stop
Or the roses of joy wither;
No more it takes than a daring hop
For our hearts to blend and glitter.

Your love will reap its cravings in heaps
And the tears of joy gently roll down
Your blood-flushed cheeks and rosebud lips
And festive you'll wear the triumphal crown.

Hurry and jump your prison wall
And leave the mournful thoughts behind
Time to heed the clarion call
And live your life and love combined.

Call me I'll come with a rosy wreath
To lay over your anxious bed
Sooner than later I'll lovingly breathe
The scent of your soul and jump ahead.

90

Let melody reign our greying age
And keep the altar flame untamed;
All pains and sorrows we'll assuage
With the song of life newly ordained.

THE WONDROUS TRAIN

Back to where the soul
Begins to gently flourish,
Back to where your heart
Throbs with mine;
The pains and sighs
shall swiftly perish
And your eyes with
Amorous delight shine.

Shame so many days
lapsed without cheer
And so many nights
Harboured hopes in vain;
Wish to feel
Your smiling lips near
And together ride
The wondrous train.

No Sweeter Arms

He recalls
First time he met you
At your conjugal home,
Full of splendour;
Adorned with taste
And glowing overview
With you serenading
Made his fancy wonder.

Time later you both
Next to each other sat
Sipping coffee and you
A mind at war revealing;
Against the pariah
Who wantonly spat
On your life with him,
No hate concealing.

You gracefully showed
brisk temptation
To tangle your heart
With a vibrant lover;
You warmed up to chant
The love oration
And taste the toxic joy
You dared rediscover.

Alas, the siren of love
Not for long blew,

And the hope of mating lips
Withered with a sigh
From your dying heart,
words silent as the dew:

*No sweeter arms
have hugged me goodbye*

SPICES AND VICES

Light, mist, heat and rain,
War, peace, love and hate
Follow one another
In the sky of memory
Of highways and byways,
Of days and years gone by.

With the wind of passion
Lighting and fanning
Flames in my mind and chest
I look for the breeze
To carry the scent and spices
Of my heart's fragrant rose
And for the wind to freeze
The vile of sardonic vices
Of people with ill will repose.

WITH RED ROSES I'LL YOU ENTHRONE

(She suffered long the bearers of greed; then sang)

I hear whispers of your bare feet
At the door of my shy retreat
Heralding your provident arrival
Unlocked, undraped, swirling
Vying to plunge into the marvel
Of florescent feeling,
Sip the fragrance of body and soul
And hum the primeval sonata,
forgetting all.

Not much more can my vision entreat.

Alas I was not there to gleam
The bliss of the joy you beam.
After long days and longer nights
Of romantic void and tedious fights
Nursing the anger and deep commotion
The bearers of greed have caused so often.
Wish I was there with you to live
Your nascent love and together give

The world away, doze and dream.

I pamper myself with hope as this
Traverse the oceans to reach the bliss
Of wondrous passion and fervent pleasure
As you radiate beyond all measure.
With red roses I'll you enthrone

And with loving soul you adorn.
Chained in hope, trusting in fate
With anxious wings I'll fly to taste

The honey enmeshed in your first kiss.

LOVE, A BIRD WITH
WONDROUS WINGS

Love is a bird with wondrous wings,
Gently perches on the soul,
The wordless tune sings
And heeds the lovers' call.

A storm may clip a sore few
Feathers from its caressing wings
Yet its wonders keep seeping through
The fragrance of its living springs.

■

BYRON TO
APHRODITE

She calls him Byron, he calls her Aphrodite

■

WHISPERS OF PASSION REBORN

*(She saw him after many years
and her passion flared anew)*

Many years were pretty hard but passed,
And so did many years of bliss;
But when my soil with his green was grassed
I blossomed like a rose on his lips.

I lay yearning upon a barren bed
Longing to whisper my reborn passion
And wild visions of lovers enmeshed
In a leaping flame beyond suppression.

In my solitary trance I cajole his new advance,
Try hard to unlock the bonds shearing my wings
And fly to his meadows to re-live romance
As a wondrous woman all sonatas sings.

SHINING IN YOUR SWEET ABODE

You are traversing the road of pain
Of sighs, of weakness, of discontent
As we all do when we cannot sustain
Galling misfortune or wounding lament.

They will not last, Dear Aphrodite.
One morning soon they will desert
Your domain and vanish out of sight
Leaving you to life's pleasures alert.

Soon in your heart new joys spring
Like white roses blossoming;
Flecked with delight in amorous mode
You'll shine in your sweet abode.

CATCHING A RAINBOW

Today I feel

I am cruising through surreal thoughts,
Gliding over rosy emotions
And nesting on a gentle heart
With a lover's melody
Weaving through my veins.

Tonight I dream

I am riding a rainbow with my soul.
There, on its lascivious banks,
I erect my temple of love
Perfumed with your fragrance
And the trance feels eternal.

At daybreak I pray

My new joy last
Until I die;
If that is too long
For Heavens to sustain
Then, at least,
Until I breathe your scent
Over a thousand starry nights.

ONE MORE CALL

Just one more call
And I'll ride the waves
To your dreaming shores
And ascend to the crest of
Your quivering passion.

I'll always you follow
Faster than my shadow
To the dreamland
Of spiced nights
Where each moment
Is primed for
Florid jubilation.

No more living rusty days,
Or traversing tortured ways.

LONG, ROSY WHILE

You landed with the stars
From high heaven
And burst my heart
Dressed in flames;
You bravely scorched
My lust thunder driven
And called me most
Endearing names.

My Phantom lover for one
Sweet Prince follows,
Such intoxicating charm,
Such grace and style
Send me entranced to roam
Your flowery meadows
And Cupid fast inspire us
For a long, rosy while.

IT'S NIGHT OUTSIDE

It's night outside and you shone again
Like a lover's kiss on kindling lips
Wearing your gown, white and loose
Flushing my heart with amorous refrain.
Erotic fragrance you showered in heaps
And set the sails of passion to cruise.

I see your eyes smiling, I see
Your cheeks aflame with dancing blood;
I feel you cruising within my veins
Caressing my soul with magic glee
And set me dreaming of a roaring flood
Sweeping us together in wondrous plains.

CUPID CALLING

The wind is howling, the rain pouring
As do our passion and ravenous kisses;
From high above Cupid calling
And blazoned we rush to grant his wishes.

I dream in my nest you gently slide
Engulfed with love you flutter and beam,
The white dress you thrust aside
And hail me sailing up the stream.

You won my heart and joyfully braced
My waves of passion and romantic air;
I won your heart and fondly embraced
Your amorous quest and erotic flare.

YOU SHONE AND BANISHED
THE WINTER

You shone and banished the winter
Of long and barren nights
And called the spring to render
The blossoms of amorous heights.

Sweet Prince looked at the meadow
And saw your charming face,
The sky in your blue eyes
And a flush in your cheeks.
Your smiles flew without a shadow
Perfuming the sunlit space;
The loneliness and pitiful sighs
Withered, no longer squeak.

Soon love swept in enthroning
Your naked jubilant heart;
Noble, sublime enchanting
Your passion to play its part.
Sweet Prince curled up, entranced
Exulting the heavenly score
And your sweetest cry romanced:
No more, No more, No more.

ENCHANTING MY SLUMBER

My blood is flowing,
My mind swamped
With the vision of the one
Enchanting my slumber;
All my senses and my passion
By her loving are trumped
And I roar saluting
Her erotic splendour.

She's engrained in the seeds
Of my heart and my soul;
She glides with
All currents in my veins;
All the gardens of romance
We happily stroll
And unlock our wants
Of all lurking chains.

SWEETER THE LOVING
RICHER THE MUSE

Loved the Freudian message you sent
To soothe my gently disguised lament
Too bold to ignore, too hot to spare
Longing to soak your loving glare.

You float on the waves of my soul
Enticing me with lustful rhapsody,
Racing passion, free of control
And eyes singing Eros' melody.

Paradise is shut, we are locked inside,
Our amorous sails are set to cruise
And when the raving on us betide
Sweeter the loving richer the muse.

DREAMS APLENTY

Dreams aplenty
When love is flying high;
If any touch the ground
The smiles joyously fly.
Aphrodite blows the siren
And Byron merrily swings
And both revel and wonder
With Eros' magic wings.

Radiant dreams will beckon
Shattering life's blips
Consoling anguished passions
With tingling amorous bliss
None will fly out the window,
Squints or quips
'Cause once their passion kindle
Not a moment they'll miss.

THE MILK OF PARADISE

We've cut the ropes
And slid into
The enchanting fields of love,
Flesh and blood
Of our thrilled bodies
Flaming with desire.

Eyes, lips, tongues, arms and thighs,
Dancing with the flames
Of our fire
And the languid murmur
Of our incessant joy.

I taste the dew
Of your opening rose
And gently inhale
The perfume
Of your beaming delight
And the nectar
Of your romantic flight.

Sunny hopes blossom in disguise
As we drink the milk of Paradise.

ALIEN WEANING WAVE

Under the winking stars
Or the smiling moon;
Under the angry sun
Or the stubborn rain,
Byron's hungry passion
Hugs the welcome boon
Of Aphrodite's loving,
Free of all refrain.

Alas the gods not always
Keen to bless the zest
Of lovers enthused
To ride the storm;
Byron's golden wish
To taste her luring breast
An alien weaning wave
Enslaved its daring form.

ANXIOUS BEAMS RE-COMBINED

Our anxious beams
Have re-combined
Sending the bashful sun
Into hiding,
Revealing the passion
Long enshrined
With laughter and kisses
Joyfully enfolding.

No more shall
the charmless silence reign
By unholy edict
Cruelly imposed.
With unyielding lips
We'll rush to taste and gain
The joy of love
In our souls reposed.

RAIN CHECK

When the heart
For love screams
And desire
Glaringly beams
No cool shower
Can ever console
Nor a rain check
Can ravish the soul.

Shine your passion
On my hungry flame
And your smile
On my fond embrace;
Cherish the ripples
Of the amorous game
And hail the loving roar
From cyberspace.

Then relax and toast
The exquisite haste
Of holding the trump card
For reaching the crest.

ODE TO APHRODITE

Drink my soul with a glass of wine
And feel my yearnings cruising to your heart;
Caress my dreams and flap your tinsel wings,
Illuminate the sky
With your toxic apparition
And rain splendour on my heart
Where orchids smile, passion repose.

Leisurely sow the lyrics of hearts newborn
And the rhythm of lovers' promenade;
You will rush to crown my sweet whispers
Touching your rosebud lips
While Eros orchestrates
The thump and throb
Of our blazing hearts.

And, in the twilight of our gleeful trance,
Eros will smile hailing our jubilant dance.

SAILING TO HEAVEN'S FURTHEST PART

We muse and chat
And sip the dreamy wine
With intimate thoughts fomenting;
Your daring looks and eager lips entwine
To spark the naked flames enchanting.

All patience abandoned
You tear the veils off your pearly breast
And hear the throbs of my anxious heart;
I kiss you east and west
And sail with you to heaven's furthest part.

CUPID SMILING ABOVE

My love has come at last
Gallantly swept my heart;
As lightning aroused me fast
And lovingly played his dart.

He calls me *my Aphrodite*,
I call him *my Byron*;
I am his soul's appetite
And he is my heart's clarion.

All with faces unseen,
And thoughts framed in love;
We hope, we yearn and lean
On Cupid smiling above.

WHIRLING IN YOUR
RIPPLING CHARMS

I long to reach
Your amorous haven
And whirl in
Your rippling charms;
Then both rise
To the seventh heaven
And wake up smiling
In each other's arms.

The whiff of the morning coffee
Allures our yearning hearts
To ascend to a fresh fantasy
Aphrodite and Byron
Rush to play their parts.

No Space for Wayward Dreams

Between lips and lips the fragrance beams
And lovers' whispers torrents breathe;
No space there left for wayward dreams
Where sweet Aphrodite removes the sheath.

No wealth, no power, no fame or cause
Can charm the soul or light the eye
More than a tameless heart where love repose
Adorned with passion and never says die.

And that's the heart sweet Aphrodite has
Enchanting Byron with shimmering play
Of flaming passion none can surpass
And delirious waves sweep and sway.

To Your Bosom I Long Aspire

To your bosom I long aspire
To feel your love and passion fomenting
And to your lips my lips desire
To breathe the toxic whispers enchanting.

The pleasure and goodness of life
Come when Aphrodite blooms and shines
Then, away vanish all worries and strife,
Our hearts will dance and our luck smiles.

Those golden days of love and zest,
And the dreamy nights of crowning bliss
We hugged and nursed high up the crest,
Will live in our hearts as one long kiss
And soon return when Aphrodite
To Byron beams her luring light.

SCENTED THOUGHTS

When parlance and verse are gently stained
  And mirthless prose is urgently sought
  The words will sound blithely strained
And passion and feelings amply distraught.

  Byron conveys his thoughts with scent
Blowing from his heart and flowering soul;
  No rocks his love for Aphrodite can dent
Nor shadows her love for Byron control.

  Let life flow on with hopes renewed
    And joy clatter when luck strikes;
  We hope, we plan, we march, we brood
  And face what comes, roses and spikes.

ALL STRANDED PASSIONS

The sails are frail, the wind is angry
And the pains are drumming the blues;
Yet the heart and the soul are hungry
For stranded passions to cruise.

Soon the sun will emit loving rays
And the moon winks and smiles abreast
Seeing Aphrodite's voluptuous forays
And Byron fondling her luscious breast.

A DANCING TALE

The Earth may be resting,
Byron's heart is not;
His passion keeps erupting
Blowing erotic what not;

Aphrodite away nursing
Dreams and roses of love dancing
In her soul, emitting bright hopes
To chuck away all ropes
And ascend to seventh sphere
With Byron singing
I've got you Dear.

DANCE WITH YOUR
AMOROUS FORAYS

Since you've dazzled my heart
And the buds of your love flowered
My verse inhaled your heart
And your joy my day dreams showered.

Now that the shadows speedily vanished
And the sun crowned our days
I'll conquer your passions ravished
And dance with your amorous forays.

I see you floating in erotic zones
Staunchly robust with inner fires,
Soon my heart with yours roams
The clear depths of sweet desires.

We climb the crest with crimson gust
And discover anew the wondrous bliss
Of dreams come true and tenderly trust
That life's pleasures we'll never miss.

THE BELLS OF JOY ARE RINGING

The bells of joy are ringing,
The birds of love are singing
On this beautifully shining day
Aphrodite's Happy Birthday.

The angels danced when you were born
A fragrant rose among the smiling daisies
With features soon in glamour shone
And passion luring the loving species.

Rise up and roam the starry sky
Of hopes you have gracefully attained
And those flying bravely high
Shall be with bliss and joy ordained.

Time won't dent your amorous soul,
Nor pains or sorrows or fake lament;
Sweet love your heart holds in control
And life's glitters without restraint.

May your romantic ripples dwell ever near
And your eyes beam the loving rays;
Through years to come I'll hold you dear
And wish you ever more Happy Birthdays.

RISE AND SHINE

The season of yoke that you befell,
Unwelcome, trampling your amorous heart,
Will soon depart leaving you jolly well
To enjoy all seasons soul-lifting art.

The moon showers the love-light fast
With you and Byron raising the mast
Of happiness throughout the starry nights
Rowing your passion with oars of delight.

MIND MAY HARDEN
WITH REASON

The mind may harden
With reason
But the heart remains
Soft and tender
Eager for loving
All seasons
And sings the joy
Of sweet surrender.

When Aphrodite
Rules the hour
Yearning, drowning
In shivering passion
Byron feels all
Her parts devour
And, elated,
They sigh and wonder.

CANNOT IMAGINE A
GREATER DELIGHT

With fiery passion I sail to your shores
The moon in your face my smiling guide;
We fuse the sparks flashing our cores
And hug the glow of erotic tide.

Cannot imagine a greater delight
Than caressing you on a roguish night
Enslaved by your seductive tongue,
Marooned with your orgasmic flight.

Not only the blue flames in your eyes,
Your honey dewed lips and pearly breast
Or your tremulous parts in satin guise
Calling to share their sweet unrest.

It's all of you, body and soul, I prize
As one we reach the mesmeric crest
And feel we've won the wondrous prize
None other hugged with greater zest.

You lay victorious, contented, whirling
In the vortex of amorous flight
The erotic glow from your eyes shining
Like diamonds in rills of moonlight.

MY HEART HAS KEENLY
YOURS SOUGHT

For weeks and weeks my heart
Has keenly yours sought
In vain 'cause you in solitude
Were forced to dwell;
I harboured hope and nursed
Tender thoughts
That soon you bid all woes
Sturdy farewell.

In my heart I built
Your warm loving nest
Thronged with red roses,
Beaming amorous tune;
Come, Dear Darling,
Perch there abreast
And see in my eyes
The smiling rays of moon.

THE SWALLOW TWITTERS
AND SINGS

A year of loving crowned our hearts
With wreaths of joy and amorous darts;
A new feeling cherished as never before
Dearly embraced and craving more.

Heart and mind and loving intense
Have lavishly combined to recompense
For the days of pain and crippling woes
Making our retreat a fragrant repose.

Your amorous calls my passion inflame
And shakes all fibres of my trembling frame;
The Swallow on my window twitters and sings
Seeing Cupid flying with fiery wings.

From distant shores I feel your flesh
Tender and warm, with mine enmesh
And feel the nectars with rapture you pour
When you ravish my jubilant roar.

CALLING PATIENCE

Come when Aphrodite's juices pour,
Come when her blossom keeps blowing,
Come when my yearning keeps glowing,
Come when memories slams my core.

Distant patience come day or night,
Help me wait for her shining light,
Grant my throbbing heart ample rest,
Until she grants me wings to her nest.

LIKE A TWINKLING STAR

Your heart is like a twinkling star,
Your spirit bright and sharp;
With steely will you've gone afar
Leaving my hope to play the harp.

Wish I can soften your tight lips
And breath the fragrance of your call;
My loving whispers will flow in heaps
And your luring voice revives the soul.

I THINK OF YOU

I think of you,
I fly naked, speechless
To your pasture;
I land on your smile
Eager to revive
Our drought-starved tango
With your fragrant embrace.

We swiftly leap dancing
To the Tunes of our hearts
As the dry roots suck
the pouring rain
And we blossom like red roses.
You are there
I am here, and
I ... think ... of ... you.

HER HEART IS A
LONE NIGHTINGALE

Hail Aphrodite reaching a roaring age
On every turn she is a glowing rage;
Wisdom and loving adorn her traits
And toxic smiles enchant her dates.

She dreams with Byron on nights of love
Laying in beds oceans apart
Wreathed with passion and poetic roses.
The smiling moon shining above
And the ecstasy, swooping their every part,
Joyfully crown their amorous prizes.

Her heart is a lone nightingale
Nesting in Byron's joyful heart,
As in paradise, happy to dwell
Chanting love songs to her sweetheart.

He toasts her and with shining eyes say:
Sweet Aphrodite, Happy Birthday.

FESTIVE SEASON'S GREETINGS

I see you perched on your couch
Delicately robed,
Looking queenly, loveable,
Curiously calm,
Silent desires fomenting,
Anxious to unfold.
A delicate smile
Adorning your charm.

I greet you with Merry Christmas
And heartfelt wishes
For a New Year crowned
With good health
And good fortune.
Me reddening your cheeks
With lover's kisses
And you floating in joy
Over the waves of Neptune.

I See Your Face
Among the Stars

Each time I sip
My favourite wine
I see your face
Among the stars and
Delicious memories
Ram anew
When nature takes
Her cue from you.

I wish you smooth
My rugged heart,
That is, I know,
Your special art
And there engrave
Your bubbly rhymes,
The spoils of wild
Wandering times.

GREETINGS TO MY
ABSENT LOVER

Dear absent love,
Heartfelt New Year wishes
Sent over the ether
With a bunch of gardenias
Heavenly perfumed, with
Love sheltered in their leaves
In thunderous silence.

May the dawn of the New Year
Shine on your soul
Vivacious melodies;
May your spirit dance
To the tunes of
Your sensuous vision
And rush to sing
The lyrics of
Hugs and kisses.

I WANDER IN YOUR
FRAGRANT SILENCE

I think of you,
Of your captive radiance
Inspiring desire
And a dream.

I wander
In your fragrant silence
Hooked to your
Riveting beam.

The wild memories
Of yesterdays
Colour my vision
In splendid ways;

Alone in my sanctum,
A cooing dove on my window,
I imagine us floating
On the waves of soothing tango.

HER LOVE IS NOT A MIRAGE

No word when the heart is cold;
No sound when memory is faint;
No poetry when crosswords take hold;
No kisses with blameless restraint.

Not romancing when the day is hot?
Not rowing when the stars are bright?
Wonder what gripped Aphrodite's slot
When Byron was flying to her delight.

He turned inward with dusky feeling
Sailing through his soul in a solitary cruise;
With troubling thoughts he faced his darling
Wondering if her love was a lit fuse.

He felt her love is real, not a passing mirage,
And her soul held his in crystal glass;
She'll soon hug him with blissful courage,
And both immerse in erotic mass.

FAREWELL SWEET APHRODITE

The Garden looked achingly beautiful,
The dove murmuring its amorous part
As Byron stood dismayed, sorrowful,
His heart struck by Aphrodite's dart
Of sudden lament, wounding, hurtful
Lauding her edict to stay apart.

Byron will nurse his injured love
And turn his longing to fancy dreams;
Will shy away from flying above
The gondola she sails in new streams
And nurse his yearning for his distant dove
With verse she used to lovingly beam.

Their love and passion not meant to be
So thinly on his vibrant soul spread;
In the twilight of her solitude she'll see
Passion-winged Byron perching on her bed,
Caressing her wants with heavenly glee
And with melodious loving they race ahead.

Over the memories with her Byron will roam,
To her fragrant bower he'll dreamily climb
And hold the reins of the intoxicating storm
Until they greet their refulgent prime
And sail jubilant in their glowing form
Through the splendour of the nights of rhyme.

For now, *farewell sweet Aphrodite*
Byron murmurs with rigid lips;
You'll remain glimmering in my sight
With incarnations of hope distance shall not clip
Neither the stars of love flash with softer light
Nor the frozen silence leads to their eclipse.

BYRON'S SOLILOQUY

Byron's thoughts are crabbed;
Under the winking moon
They sail to your name
And see the mosaic of stars
Reflect your desires
Galloping from star to star
In your new private universe.

Look into the mirror
Not through the window.
You'll see what you love most
To be, to do,
To have, to give, to feel.
If you see him
Flying in your universe
Flapping the wings of a swallow
Raise the toast of love
And he'll acclaim
The marriage of heart and soul
In the meadows
He and you together stroll.

If he's not in your mirror flapping,
Or just surfacing and fading,
Then look through the window,
See the transient coloured existence
Of all living creatures
Captive in the cycle of life and death
Revolving, inexorably
By will or stealth.

With tired fascination
You may retire
Into your dreaming bed,
Read the love poetry
Of the poet you savour
And hear Byron's surreal voice
Whispering to your erotic impulse.

You turn page after page
Trying to escape
Its beguiling resonance
And deny your romantic opulence;
But, unlike Houdini,
You cannot undo
The shackles of his memory
Or your Cupid's armoury.

Byron deserted your universe
'Cause you drove a silent sword
Through his heart,
His soul, his pride,
So suddenly, so ruthlessly;
As if you've never
Wallowed in his embrace,
Or hummed
The lovers' grace.

As if you've never consumed his fire
With your eloquent lips,
Or forced his surrender
With dazzling flips.

As if he has never fluttered
In your amorous rhyme
Or any verse he has uttered
Worth a dingy dime.

Times he imagines
You are sucked
Into a new vortex of lust;
Not just
Touring the meadows
Of romantic crust.
Worry not, silent Aphrodite,
He can wear his scars
As gladiatorial bars
And render his sorrow
A tongueless sparrow.

No, not you becoming
Uninhabited island
In the middle
Of turbulent solitude.
Your image
Shall tantalisingly remain
Tattooed in his soul
And your voice
Vibrating in his domain
Beyond control.

If it's an offence or fault
Kept you silent
Just say the word
And he'll jealously redeem.

If it's woes of health
And pain strident
May the gods rid them
As a feeble dream.
Not you to suffer
Grey, restless discontent,
Pains, monotony
Or the void of lament.

May the red wine of your choice
Glow brightly in your cheeks
And the tune of love in your voice
All your desires warmly streak.

If one day fate decrees you ring the bell,
and the rosy ferns of your passion unfurl,
All Byron's dormant woes will evaporate
And, with hungry insatiable lips,
he'll lovingly quip:
Sweet Aphrodite, welcome home.

THAT IS MY DREAM

To fling my arms wide
Where sunrays vibrate,
To whirl and to dance
Till my passion oscillate,
Then welcome the evening
And breathe the roses blue
While night comes on gently
Inspiring like you

That is my dream.

To fling my arms around you
In the face of the smiling moon,
Dance, whirl, caress
And feel your passion boon
Galloping from lip to lip
Eager to thrill the hour
While the stars keep twinkling
And you my passion devour.

That is my dream.

WE LOVE, WE ASPIRE, WE INSPIRE

The wings of time flutter, never tire
We live its creak, its crunch, all its ways;
Yet we love, we aspire and inspire.

I sip the red wine on this lucky day
When you gently shine a glittering ray
And warmly wish me Happy Birthday.

SMILING FIRES

We've hanged our untamed desires
On crimson hopes and scarlet patience
Knowing the sunrise of our smiling fires
Will trump the meddling of the arid silence.

Drink my soul in a glass of red wine
And caress my passion with your drunken lips;
The rays of joy will from your eyes shine
And the flowers of loving blossom in heaps.

Wish to swiftly fly to your dreamy nest,
And wrap you with elixirs of my yearning;
Breath the fragrance of your supple breast
And see in your eyes desires swirling.

■

REFLECTIONS

■

THE FINAL RING OF LIFE'S BELL

Luck smiles to those who smile,
Stars twinkle to those who dream,
The nightingale sings to those in love.
And lovers reaching the climax scream.

But when the brain is shut in the cage of woes,
Passion frozen in the fridge of desires,
And sprinklers of loving are turned off
The flickers of yearning will sink in mires.

And when windows of hope are firmly shut
And the doors of solitude are locked,
Life will soon become little more than
Flesh and bones on silent beds docked.

Awaiting the final ring of life's bell
Wondering what have we left at the altar of sorrow?
What gain we reaped in shuffling through the gloom?
What blessed things we leave for tomorrow?

IT'S NOT ALL SWEET DELUSION

Is there a joy fate can give
Like the one it takes away
Leaving strangled hopes perceive
Shadows of bloom fading away?

No, it's not all sweet delusion;
The glow of love flashing from the eyes
And the passions soaring in fiery fusion
Long shall be treasured as heavenly prize.

KISSES HOST THE RAINBOW
AFTER RAIN

Her soul is imprisoned by her remorseless loss
Of love, libido, youthful dreams and Cupid's wings
That carried her exquisite passion swiftly across
All barriers to what made her heart happily sing.

She lays in the shade of the graces he's bestowed
In his heart and his soul when together they sailed
In the gondola of love with delight enthralled
Awaiting the new rays of her passion regained.

Why suffer the long lonely ride on the train
Of life thinking old joys are forever lost
And look old and sour as if never again
The rays of joy dissolve the layered frost?

A hug can smooth the sufferers' stubborn pain
And a kiss can host the rainbow after rain;
The clouds cannot shut out the stars all the time
Nor sorrow the love and glare of lovers' prime.

He laid bare his hope
on the rays of the sun
And she laid bare her woes
On the rocks of despair;
Would they again be crowned
With good luck and run
To where nightingales and doves
Sing their love affair??

THE SIREN OF THE HEART

The siren of the heart keeps blowing
Alas, no echo sliding from the hills;
No butterflies fluttering
To brighten the greyness of his dream;
No flowers diffusing the fragrance
To enliven the soul.
Would she ever call?

He imagines her
A phantom of delight;
Beautiful eyes
Like twilight stars;
A heart dancing;
A silent waterfall
Of emotions reverberating,
Warm, comforting, commanding.
And wishes he wakes up
To see her... smiling.

HUMANITY UNREDEEMED

Adam and Eve the apple ate
And merrily leapt to procreate.
The Prophets since and Godly kings,
Built up virtue on the swings.

Poets followed, scientists and philosophers,
Sketched the world and the living in avid colours
While serpents of hate and greed kept crawling,
Mauling virtue, love and peace, ever mauling.

Holy books, pious sermons, graceful bands,
Shed God's wisdom and commandments on the sands,
Then blown asunder by gusts of evil and hungry ego,
Leaving haters and power hungry free to tango.

No gun, no sword or angry spear
Brought us durable peace any near.
Like white stars we fade away
Leaving hopes lamenting the day.

If roses could speak and wickedness vanish
With evil thoughts draped in melodious sound
The house of life will in happiness flourish
And people would be by goodness bound.

Look into your heart, mind and soul,
See if love and reason there cajole;
If so all men on this unthinking earth
May bond in peace and norms of worth.

THE FUTURE TURNS PAST

History shows and more of late,
Merchants of evil, greed and hate,
Serpents of war, oppression and death
And satans   disguised as angels of wealth
See no sun, no stars, no rainbow, no moon,
To lighten the virtue of peace and boon.

The history of faith and morals is short,
And goodness, though worthy, never will last,
Nature and humans shall life abort,
And sooner or later the future turns past.

THE UPRISING

(Following the Uprisings in Egypt in 2011,
and subsequently in Tunisia and Libya)

Against the blank of rights and law
They will not sing praises
Or raise red and white roses.
The sirens of fury run high and low.

The Eaglehawks are dangling
With wings ungallantly shorn;
Their last breath is hanging
By a thread of tortured scorn.

Will pigeons and angels fill the space
Of pious words and naked want?
Or Tiger Snakes will creep in place
And hiss the venom with sugared font?

BEFORE THE MAGIC ENCOUNTER

The plane spread its wings
High up where no demons hunt
Or angels wallow in love.
The fervent hopes of seeing her at long last
Raided his heart like victorious chevaliers;
Fears of missing her whirling in his head
Like a treacherous eddy in midocean.

There, in the void under the bright blue sky,
He imagines her moonlit beauty
Caressing the stars,
Her smiling eyes
splashing erotic vows
And her naked body
hovering over the bonfire
Ignited with blood and passion
Waiving to him the rose he gave her
In his dream, the night before he flew.

He lands, his hopes refreshed;
His fears eclipsed by her enchanting image;
The Princess of love and ecstasy,
The Mistress of tenderness and grace.

He day dreams leafing through
The rainbow pages of their magic encounter
On the Seine embankment
Where lovers are never shy;
On the topmost girder of the Eiffel Tower
Where the amorous spirit hovers ever higher.

What else can he dream of things to creep
Other than seeing her smiling in her sleep?

BEMOANING THE INSOLENT FATE

He hovered close over her meadows,
Hopes blooming and togetherness
Greening in brimful melody.
From skies far away
He saw her gorgeous radiant face
And goodness flushing her grace.

Alas, fate portended otherwise;
The church bells stopped ringing.
He felt his wings shorn,
His planned date withered
And the eager encounter with his dove
Faded upon the naked earth.

Tears clouded his vision,
His face, solemn, cold, forlorn,
Stared into the void;
No hope easing his distress,
No consoling Princess.

He wallowed in his solitude,
Bemoaning the insolent fate
Clouding the dream of
Seeing the flush in her cheeks,
Feeling the flutter in her passion,
Relishing the seduction in her smile and
The insane fate preventing them
Sheltering in each other's arms
Where amorous passions reside
And toxic desires stride.

He sought her forgiveness and,
With rays of new hope radiating,
He iterated his belief that
The ship of life not always plainly sails
Nor does it always reach its port;
But a candid dream mercifully prevails
And life pleasures speedily hails.

THEY LEAVE ASIDE THE
SORDID CLOCKS

He misses her lush vibrant bed
And the fragrance of her breast;
He craves the dry tears she sheds
Soon as she reaches the blazing crest.

When they rise up and happily flush
The nascent dawn with loving smiles;
No nagging torment or caution to brush
Nor fingers whirling in gyres of riles.

Back to where the soul begins to gently flourish
Back to where the heart throbs with a loving kiss
Where pains and angst swiftly perish
And love showers the beams of heavenly bliss.

They leave aside the sordid clocks
Rushing the time best left frozen
And scatter all dormant hopes
As withered leaves out of season.

He dreams her eyes with affection shine
When the sea and the sky are blue
And his vibrant passion and want combine;
Out of sight out of mind—how untrue.

MEMORIES

When he sees the breeze
Gently sways the white sails
Of the yachts of lovers in the sea
She quickly rides the waves of his soul
And banks on the shores of his dreams
Where the rainbow crowns her beauty
And the lilies dance with her beams.

Long he impatiently lingered
His heart drumming the blues,
Venting dauntless hopes
To regain the precious lost prize
Waiting for the bell to ring
And for the nightingale to sing
The song of love in candle light.

THE CALIPHATE OF APOSTASY

The pristine simplicity, the egalitarianism
humanism, justice and sanctity of life
reigning at the times of the prophet of
Islam, Mohammad Bin Abdullah (PBUH)
and his succeeding four Caliphs, save for his
committing the atrocity of beheading more
than six hundred men and pubescent boys
and the enslavement of the women and
children of the Jewish tribe of Qurayzah,
turned, under the Caliphate of
Abu Baker Al Baghdadi,
the self-appointed 21st Century Caliph,
to murderous zealotry, pious brutality, venomous
sermonising and naked apostasy.

This 2014 Caliphate named The Islamic State of Iraq and
the Levant (ISIL), which occupied the northern
part of the fertile land where the Tigris and the
Euphrates Rivers fertilised the Babylonian
wealth and culture for centuries, turned into a sworn enemy
of civil liberties and denier of law and order.

ISIL became the Caliphate of Apostasy,
The theatre for preachers of pious brutality,
Marauders devoid of any trace of humanity,
Vultures sick for battle
Tyrants the innocent throttle.

The land where by force they perch
Became the stage where eagles lurch;

Killers enjoy beheading,
Warped beliefs spreading
Diffusing venom without disguise
Aiming to reach the illusive paradise.

Great shame ISIL mature pragmatism abandoned
Blind hallmark and immutable dogmatism cordoned
While Muslims elsewhere enjoy religious pragmatism,
Pluralism, mutual respect and civil humanism.

ISIL's pulse may yet for a while vibrate
But doomed it will by its actions disintegrate;
The lions of freedom will catch its tyrants in their paws
And the leopards of justice gnaw them in their jaws.

They'll become splinters of flesh and bone
Crawling on the dust of their throne
Tottering on the edge of oblivion
With no grieving communion.

The Caliphate of Apostasy will die away;
No such other will see the light of day.

GREVIOUS DEEDS SEALED HER FATE

In her arid soul flowers never flourished
And the scars in her body are the emblem of disgust;
Her deceitful face of anguish always sought
New believers her vicious whiles to trust.

She dropped out of life into misery went
Where doctors aplenty and law eagles frequent
Shovelling her pain, fretting her burning anger
Mouth dribbling complaints, in woes wander.

She dwells with anger, pills and pain
Hugging distress but chasing gain.
Bereft of joy, of hope, of peace
Engulfed with doubt, seldom at ease.

The man she loved left her to Heaven's care
With scattered weeds of goodness left to stew;
The tender vows she made to cherish her love affair
Are dead and buried, none will shine anew.

Never faith has so wantonly broken
Nor love so blithely demeaned;
She dwells in solitude, all mores shaken
And of all recantations weaned.

Her grievous deeds sealed her fate
Long for her salvation she'll lie in wait,
And when her soul will in despair leave
Hundreds will mourn but none will grieve.

THE SPRING ADORNED
HIS OBSESSION

She cut his heart with jagged words
And left him sunk in mid-stream;
He knew not why the singing birds

Suddenly blustered his whirling dream
Of seeing her frizzled in his passion
And lovingly dandled her longings beam.

The spring adorned his obsession
And the daffodils sang with glamour;
His mermaid reclaimed the rugged ocean

With vacant lips he heard her murmur:
"One swallow does not make a summer".

WHISPERS OF DAWN

(After reading Adibeh Attia's poetry compendium
"Whispers of Dawn" and listening to her recitation)

I loved your Whispers of Dawn
And clung to your emotive reading.
The hearts that are forlorn
Drown in your hungry pleading
And those that are with wine blown
Sway in your whispers reeling.

Time with you galloped with glee
Trumping the fabulous, wonderful lunch.
As poets we feel our souls are free
And rush with whispers all worries to crunch.
We relish the smiling moon to see
And make of beauty and love a delicious punch.

LAMENTATIONS

MY SMILING ANGEL

(Badly hurt by one, deeply loved by another)

Alone I lay cowered in awe,
Feeling my soul rant and blow,
'Cause one uncouth with thwarted mind
Stabbed me and left his shadow behind
Prowling down the valley of hate,
Harmful, unworthy, moaning his fate.

The pains I still endure, the pills I often gulp,
The needles I procure, the perils I try to jump;
Days and nights no end, aches and pains they pile,
Yet all hardly matter once I see you smile.

Up on my life's ladder or down the slope,
You are the one to cuddle and charm my hope.
I wish no fortune, no praise, no power,
Your love alone is my sole desire.

Thunder and rain, hail and sunshine,
I seek your heart as my nursing shrine.
No greater joy can redeem my soul
Than being with you in love stroll.

Alone with you I light the candle,
I play the music and stop the time;
I challenge fate, courage handle
And with wounded wings I reach my prime.

In quickened breath I mount the throne
Of passionate love with you alone

And reach up high to seventh heaven
Where true love is by Angels driven.

Away you flew too far my love
And left my heart beseeching;
My yearnings burst the sky above
Your glowing stars entreating.
Fly back to me, my smiling angel,
Whisper your love and light the candle.

I SAY TO PAINS FAREWELL

The night came, ghost like, hazy
Hugging memories of intimate scent,
The stars are tame, the breeze lazy,
Nudging a heart that won't relent.

Hers is a dancing hope,
In the valley of yearning,
Passion that won't elope,
Thoughts and patience burning.

Wished time comforts her love,
Waiting, dreaming, longing,
And send him the beautiful dove,
With rosy message singing.

Why she loves him? Seasons of reasons erupt,
Of none she told him, 'cause telling may corrupt
Feelings deeper than oceans can boast
And fragrance richer than Eden can host.

The love she promised to hold dear,
The vows she swore to keep him near
Glittered his pride as the lucky man,
The only one she craves under the sun.

Say not farewell, him she implored,
none more a heartless hurtful word,
Shutting my singing love in a hermit's cell.
Embrace my heart, keep my passion stirred,
'Cause only with you I say to woes farewell.

WITH YOU MY DAYS
WILL BRISKLY FLY

*(Long suffered, she challenged the
odds and embraced a new love)*

Take me to the hills of hope
Where the celestial lights oscillate,
Where untamed passions elope
And all desires vibrate.

I've seen life's worst and
Man's beguiling ugliest;
Then heard the silver clarion's call
Attention to the loveliest.

Wish I forgot him who hurt me
Weary, wasted, worn he left me,
No remorse, no qualms or pangs
On his conscience nothing hangs.

May the brand of Cain
On his forehead remain
Till he would recantation write
For the wrongs he cannot right.

Unrepentant, unashamed, pride driven,
Unperturbed with his guilt unforgiven;
For years to come the bloodstain
On his conscience shall remain.

Like a rudderless bark in alien waters
I drifted, soaking the frothy spray

Until I berthed at your shores
And felt I hardly need to pray.

Let those who love to brawl and fight
Waste the sunny glorious days,
And miss to cuddle the starry night
In many sweet beautiful ways.

My loss was great, so was my prime,
Now with you my heart beats sublime;
Hug me, kiss me, turn my cheeks rosy red
And feel our souls have long been wed.

With head erect by the pond I walk,
With love I beam, of love I talk;
Alive and merry with wings spread out
I leave the qualms to those who doubt.

I challenged the odds, no longer I go
Uphill, nor shall my tears flow;
I fairly earned a season of rest
And rose to love and reached the crest.

Man of virtue, man of merit, man of care,
Hold me close, let me feel your magic flair;
Let's fly, lip on lip, by love driven
Wrapped with joy to seventh heaven.

Be you my breeze, my wings, my sky
My shield in days of heavy rain,
With you my days will briskly fly
No groans, no thorns, no groaning pain;

With teeming passion and dazzling eye
Unlock my shackles and never wane.

You and I, my love, must run
Along the plains and up the hills,
Breathe the scent of life as one
And cleave to all that rocks and thrills.

THE EMPRESS OF SURVIVAL

*(Several times she sought oblivion for the distress she suffered;
then renaissance beckoned in a chance encounter)*

He cut me up
He quashed me down
Then smiled in self esteem
Like a clown in mid-stream.
The sun drowned inside me;
No more dawns in my world
Any more.

The truth I sought
I found dead;
Slain in the head of
The dissector of organs and souls;
Sowing pain and misery
And boasting
Of being human.

Doomed I am to remember
His blood-stained cross
And ache to forget.
O' truth will you ever
Come back to life
And wipe out the agony
Carved on my flesh,
'Cause I want
To forgive.

Thrust in the darkness of despair
I embraced it thrice

Gulping pills of extinction
Seeking eternal rest
To no avail.

Doomed to live,
To nurse my pains,
Suffer the thorns
Stuck into my heart
By kith and kin I loved
And became caricatures
Of my own flesh and blood.

Please God
Stop me living in pain,
In anger.
Let me rest
On the grass of contentment
Free of hate, of vengeance.
I crave for painless life.

Alone I move
With rippled moods
Slowly, in roaring silence
Like a dark cloud
In the far horizon.
I dwell in emptiness,
In silence.

Alone in my glorified prison
Called home,
Where only the caressing songs
Of my singer of yester years,

Lamentations

Temper my loneliness,
Excite intimate memories
And make me feel,
For a precious moment,
That I am still a woman
Longing for love.

How much longer
Shall I sustain
The noxious bondage
To the man
I once hugged in matrimony?

How much longer
Shall I sink
Into the corrosive depth
Of undying hurt?

How much longer
Shall I condemn
The irreversible travesty
To my body?
How much longer
Shall I pray
for the revival
Of my soul?

All appears endless.
I need my own Wailing Wall
To drown with my tears
And entrust with the wish

I have written
With trembling fingers:

Please God, shut
The book of my suffering
And crown my sky
With the rainbow of joy.

You came
From nowhere;
A sparrow, fluttering
In the vacuum of my universe.
You held me
In your gentle arms,
Wrapped me with
Your tender smile and,
As in fairy land,
The honey flowed
Over my lips
As I dived into the sea
Of longing.

Before you shone in my sky,
Whenever I turned towards hope
It vanished like a phantom
In a deserted island.

I needed you, my Sparrow
To unmask the glitters
Of my sanity,
To rekindle the flickering flame
Of my passion;

Hoping, I would revisit happiness,
Enjoy the raindrops on my face and
Sleep, sleep
Without pain killers,
Without insomnia killers,
Without distress killers
And wake up, beside you
Feeling your fingers
gently fossicking the hair
On my dreaming head.

The melody of your heart,
The magic of your touch,
Flow through my veins and
Animate my soul.
With you, my Sparrow
The weariness of my layered distress,
And the darkness haunting my vision
Fade into outer space.
My body, my soul
Plunge into a pool of serenity
To the depth of subliminal joy.

My Prince of Comfort,
Play for me the tunes of intimacy,
Hold me with your warmth,
Inflame my passion with
The spark of your eyes,
Fill my soul with
The fragrance of your love and
Let me smile and whisper
I *love you*.

I know where I came from;
I do not know,
Or wish to know
My new destination.
I shall hoist a green banner
On the pole above my new life.
The dark clouds of yesterday
Will pass it by
Leaving no shadow.
No bleak dawns,
No starless nights.

The morning breeze of spring
Will diffuse
The fragrance of your love
Into my veins
In caressing, intimate melody.

My birthday is coming.
Pain has abandoned me.
I am stepping on
The threshold of a new life,
Tossed into the waves
Of a daring cruise to
the unknown.

I wish to live up to
My new unknown;
No gifts
No cards
No parties.

The rhapsody of your heart
And the tenderness of your touch
Will be the celebration
Of my rebirth,
The New Me:

The Empress of Survival.

JESSAMINE OF MY HEART

*(Father addressing his daughter, the Mermaid, after she left
with her husband, the Sailor, and infant daughter leaving no
shadow behind)*

The Sailor
Lowers the sails of his odyssey
Drops the anchor of mythology
Lands in the valley of content
Embraces the Mermaid
With effervescent portent and
With a beautiful daughter,
A new trinity is born.

The anchor with her parents
Is severed
By a tidal wave.
The ship drifts away
In the alluring light
Of new horizons.

The Mermaid serenades on
The rocky coast of discovery,
The wide embankment
Of love and
Rests at the foot of a bridge
Watching, once in a while,
On the far side
The images of her parents and
The wanderings of her brothers
Hoping

The trees would beam,
The rocks scream,
The wells overflow
And the birds sing Hallelujah.

Alas, all on the far side
Appear motionless,
Stolid, desolate
Save for the whispers
Of a lone sparrow
In lament and sorrow

The Mermaid turns back,
Expectations betrayed
The salt of anger
Mixed with fragments of love
Clutching to the spikes of
Disappointment and
Indifference.

Distant Mermaid,
Not me
Sit, wait, judge, condemn
Seek or suffer dominion.
My thoughts, my emotions
Run faster than my feet
Yet, I cannot reach your retreat.
You dwell in the eternal,
I in the temporal.
The Maker I have deserted
Is now your Father illuminating

Your spirituality, your marriage,
Your motherhood, your independence.
I became a silent verse
In your adopted universe.

Wish I could fly
To your colourful sky,
Feel the silvery rays
Of beauty and warmth
Of your new trinity,
Dance to your radiating happiness
And erase my sheltered scar.

Change much as you like,
Live your life, roam or hike
Whether, in the flutter of events and
The oscillations of our journeys,
You and I
Flock in harmony, or drift apart
You will remain
The Jessamine of my heart.

ALONE YOU SUFFER
THE SILENT BLITZ

(She muddied his love and sank into sorrowful solace)

No wealth, no honour, no joy or domain,
While love and virtue absent remain,
Wreaths of thorns will crown the days,
Of those who cling to hurtful ways.

Love in your heart not in comfort sits
Alone you suffer the silent blitz
Of solitude wrapped in smiling disguise,
Of cravings quashed by pills of surmise.

Nights adorned with eyes bulging,
Solace aching, worries nagging,
Deep sorrows and complex wiles,
Blame and tears and absent smiles.

You muddied the sweet water of life
And sipped the salt water of strife;
You lament misfortune as a vile flame
And hum the tunes of curse and blame.

Your gloomy soul, and amoral deeds,
Turned your wayward yearns to a rocky heap
And the flowers of love to shredded weeds.
Who would into your dark bosom creep?

CHAMPION OF BETRAYAL

(When matter eclipsed morals)

Despaired she sought oblivion
In vain 'cause always survived
To hear the roaring clarion
To wars for gain contrived.

Years of anger, pain and blood,
Coloured her mores and thoughts in mud,
Eyes of despair with malice slept,
And loyalty and love were blithely swept.

She met the man she felt she knew
For years and years and felt within
Resurgent love flowering anew,
And sought his heart keenly to win.

And win she did his heart and care
And thought they were from heaven rare;
Her waves of passion eclipsed the score
With tearful joy and sweet uproar.

She lights the candle and sings of love,
And dances with him in amorous motion;
Lips to lips rush and the stars above,
Diffuse the scent of swirling passion.

Fondly she says the morning after
How sweet and serene she tenderly slept,
The joy, the warmth and the shy decanter
To her pains and anguish a knockout dealt.

The scars she had in shame concealed
So gently he touched and subtly revealed;
Her passion beamed and all veils shoved,
And ravished the touch she dearly loved.

His heart became her only claim,
His bond she sought with deep acclaim;
For a while he thought she climbed the crest,
And dumped the woes that saddled her chest.

Her feathered nest they warmly fared
And lived a dream in blessed seclusion;
They talked of love, emotions flared
And rays of passion showered the fusion.

Life for her not meant for long to enjoy;
Phantoms of grievance and demons of hurt
Returned to feed her bent to blame, to destroy
The love long cherished she smothered with dirt.

All that his healing touch warmly bettered
Her tormented soul ungainly shattered.
For a transient gain of a lowly worth
She tore the heart of life's mirth.

The Empress turned a cat, cunning all her own,
One prey can hardly her hunger blunt.
The jaws of wayward zeal haunt her at dawn
And triumphs in mauling the prey she hunts.

Sculpted in clay, bereft of mores,
She hugs her faith in godless shrine;

With hollow heart on deserted shores
She celebrates her soul's fast decline.

She cut the cord with sudden chop;
No words of sorrow or gentle farewell;
No shame to efface the treacherous flop,
No ripples of vows she sang so well.

Shame the faithful mauls the faithless
And prays to earn the bliss of Eden;
All that's precious she rendered worthless
And the wreaths of morals with thorns laden.

Farewell, he said, with silent words,
I leave you to your heaven's care.
The dream of wingless limping birds
Will haunt your nights, your days ensnare
And the amorous touching, the erotic flair,
Will pain your heart for a loving mate.
All memories with you will in sorrow glare
And the love you battered crown your fate.

THE ANGELS WITNESS
MY SORROW

(Voice of repentance)

Weeks and months in silence rolled
As my soul was breathing fire,
Steadily, vainly I ignored
The swarming waves of hot desire.
Betrayed the love I have enthroned
And cruelly dumped in distant mire.

No sweets or wine jogged my space
Or wit and laughter crossed the gloom;
The worldly gains fattened my case
But missed the meadow where roses bloom.
Your wondrous love and warm embrace
Swept my fate with spiky broom.

I know not why I profaned my love
And held the hands that badly hurt you;
The tears I've shed the Angels above
Witnessed in sorrow, far deep and true.
My daring hope to reclaim your love
Remains sublime; would it brew?

TRAMPLING OVER A
THROBBING HEART

Weeks and months rolled in silence
And nagging hope shrank to naught;
He dearly wished she'll bridge the distance
And embrace a tender thought
Freeing her wants from thorns and thistles
And seek his love when passion whistles.

She treads the cobwebbed path of war
And burn her veins chasing shadows;
Undermining every score
Just to keep exhaling sorrows.
Silent, pensive, searching, restless
Tired, worn yet always huntress.

Much he loved her dreaming glances
Much she prized his fond embrace;
With zest they took their daring chances
And leapt to glow in frenzied pace.
Always craved the unholy flirt
With naked flesh in smiling mirth.

She smothered the love she cherished
And left her lover nursing his ire;
Preferred to bury the ghost she ravished
And sink into the warring mire.
With wailing heart and harried looks
She nestled in her woeful nooks.

Hard to fathom what possessed her
Trampling over a throbbing heart
In vain he tried to release her
From pains and woes her ghost imparts
Yet she offered not a single rose
To show a sign of veiled remorse.

With all the lights of love turned off
Her soul was doomed, her steps accursed;
Yet she still appeared as toff
But her heart and mind gamely dispersed
Nothing but germs of greed and brawl
Leaving no space for Satan to prowl.

When love is perjured and faith blown
The nights turn grey, the days weary;
The bed where love brilliantly shone
Turns to icy cold rock, dreary
And the cheers and bubble of life
Become gloomy languid strife.

NIGHTLY TEARS

She lives her daily dramas
And sheds her nightly tears
Adrift with shattered illusions
And heart enmeshed in fears.

Surrounded by trammels of woe
Oppressed with shams of rectitude;
Her wealth encased in pain and awe
The Puppy alone adorns her solitude.

With the spell of her fancy broken
And her quest for love ensnared
She lost her romantic token
And the fire within despaired.

She had to follow the canard
Of nobility and moral pretence
Integrity became a hazard
And decency abject offence.

She hit him hard, by greed commanded,
Knowing too well he'll be deeply hurt,
Grace and shame her soul deserted
And the roads to loving badly burnt.

You Speak of the Awes

You speak of the awes
Your son on you inflicted;
Of the ghosts haunting
The scary dreams you breed;
Of the ills and the deaths
Week on week persisted
All of which stopping
Your love to be freed
And leaving you with
Memories of the lover
You have rushed with
A blazing heart to discover
Feeling thirsty for a whisper,
For a hug, for a roar
Feeling hungry for the touch
To be sated evermore.

Yes, you speak of desire to farewell
All the pains cramped over your soul
And the worries you can hardly control,
Then you slide back, exhausted, to your shell
Play the songs that console your restless heart
And feel the breeze of the love that won't depart.

LOVE STRANGLED

He listened to your sorrowful tales,
To the pulse of your bitterness
And he weighed you in human scales
At the gates of loving tenderness.
The moon shone on your merry sails
Soon you landed on rousing wilderness.

Recall when you undress by the quivering candlelight?
Shedding the layers of all holy covers
And stretch out nude, cluttering, cheeks alight
With untamed lust and sweet uproarious shudders.

Now, maligned, you live sterile days, relatives dying
Their corpses lowered with wolves crying;
Wake up, burst out of your sordid womb
Before the smiling flowers crowd your silent tomb.

All sweet memories of yester love
Withered in your moonless cage;
Alone beseeching the Lord above
And nesting sorrows and silent rage.

Say not farewell to love you suddenly strangled;
Shed no tears bewailing its fate;
Your pains and sorrows have happily mingled
Life is short, you say, so let's forget.

If ever you feel regret, recanting
Go back to him, naked, if he's alive;
He'll take you to the woods new love hunting
With gaping wounds and sullen, staggered drive.

HE CAME FLYING

He came flying
Bearing magnolias in his heart;
Furious blood steering his way
Beyond reason, beyond wine,
Beyond terrestrial woes,
Beyond shadows of fear.
No doubts him pursued,
No clouds his vision dented.

He came flying
Over the ocean of yearning
Hearing only your tender vibes,
Seeing you sheltered
In your sordid castle,
Dressed like a bereaving actress,
Surrounded by wreaths of cement
Coiled inward with vigorous lament.

He perched up the tree of hope,
Blew the horn of yearning
Hoping you'll open the gates,
Flap your wings and, together
Rule the sky with brazen passion
And roaring ecstasy.
Alas, the gates remained shut,
His hopes by sorrow beset
And his heart filtering regret.

You have soaked many seasons
With unholy tears,

Hoping to unearth a petal of grace,
A nugget of happiness
To console your tortured soul.
Alas, no petal smiled,
No nugget shined.
All vanished with your tears
And horror dreams
Into the unknown
Where your avarice and betrayal
Ungainly reside.

Recall when a hug, and a kiss
And a tune of love
Glittered the passion in your eyes,
Lit the candle of your romance
And you lay with him
Smothered with the perfume of ecstasy,
Crowned with the gardenias of joy
And rising up looking victorious
Beaming with a conqueror's smile?

Alas, the gates of your sordid castle
Remained shut;
His hope to hear you chant
A word of sorrow,
A quest to forgive,
A desire to shed tears of joy
Faded into the unknown.

He went back, a dark umbrella
Covering his regret and
The moaning magnolias.

THE GRACELESS SON, KILLER OF LOVE

(Addressing her son)

For nine months I nurtured you in my womb,
For years you sucked my loving care;
Alas, your sinful greed made you a vice groom
Bereft of virtue, no grace to spare
And no love to cheer your sullied gloom.

You dabbled your sleek hands in my soul
Aiming to grab what's left of my belongings;
You scoffed at my signs of control
And cherished hurtful abusive scolding.

That's when you came raging, foaming splashing
Insults, kicking, slapping, inflicting dreadful pain,
And ever since I left you your froth gushing
With your dignity and manhood down the drain.

You crushed the mother's love in my breast
As you crushed my ageing feeble ribs
With unblessed hands and villainous quest
And hailed your shabby victory with dark fibs.

What could a mother do to a wayward son
Immersed in the den of vice and sin
Who frowns even when a fortune won
Strangers to him are kith and kin.

Drooping with no speck of approbation,
A placid miscreant, a shrivelling wreck,

Swathed with black coat of mortification
And sank in vice up to his sullied neck.

Adorned with hollow looks and haggard parts,
Immersed in the soot of polluted bonds
And crooning the melody of wretched hearts
Played by miscreants and ravenous blonds.
You caused me unbearable anguish and pain
I swear I'll never be your mother again.

HEAVING LAMENT

He waited and waited
Heaving lament
Holding at bay
His stubborn desire;
No sign, no whisper
Of sweet consent,
No chanting lips
To cool the fire.

Bemoaning the fate
Of the injured bloom,
The tunes of love
And the rosy faces
Shall not scatter
Her ravishing perfume
Or stop him hailing
Her dawning aces.

LOST HIS SMILING FACE

He rang you,
Your phone didn't speak;
He forgot his smile;
Urged by his addiction to
Your laughter,
He rang you again.

He only heard
Melancholic tingling.
He forgot he was
A salamander
Meandering in your fire.
Those sordid sounds,
Like ice drops
Doused his hopes.

His dove didn't flutter.
He lay down the phone and
Lost his smiling face.

HER RAVISHING CHAIN

Is there no limit to her love in this world?
Hasn't it got a sleeping lid?
A volcano would have subsided;
A waterfall exhausted;
Even a devil can turn merciful.
No, her love is fire parading in her veins,
Its fragrance perfumes the air she breathes,
Its chains ravish her soul;
Its coolness kills her patience
Its pains are tasteful.

She'll cling to it even if she knew
It will bring forth her end
And embrace it as her last fort.
All songs pale compared to its chant;
No violin emits a nicer tune.
Fate does not rule it
No wealth makes her grateful.

Who in his wisdom or ignorance
Is able to deny love
Crowning his heart?
In its nest it feeds you
The honeyed vibrations of life
In its absence?
The poison of solitude.

CELEBRATIONS

Effervescent, Superfine

*(Recited at the celebration of my wife Judith's
69th Birthday at the home of our friends
Joe and Rachelle Rosenberg)*

At the age of something-nine,
You look as young as forty-nine
Animating as red wine
Effervescent, superfine;
May well be counted as divine
Thank heavens you are mine.

The love, the hopes, the joy we share
And all the beautiful friends around
Make all the weights easy to bear
And all the bonds strong and sound.

We drink with those who care
And laugh with those who drink
And dance no matter where
And wink to those who blink.

Raise your glasses high and say
To you, Dear Judy, Happy Birthday;
You look as young as yesterday
And never stops to fly away;
The sculptures you make,
The Bridge you play
To world acclaim
Shall pave the way.

Thank you, Rachelle and Joe
For making such a splendid show
Clothed with grace, crowned with glow
From your hearts the goodness flow.
May your fortunes grow and grow
And blessed we be with your 'Hallo'.

A NIGHT TO REMEMBER

*(On the occasion of Ola and Geoffrey
Cohen's 50th Wedding anniversary)*

It's time to remember,
On eleventh of December,
Nineteen hundred and fifty-seven,
Ola and Geoffrey were joined in Heaven.

Hallelujah friends and all,
Hope you heed the Cohen's call,
To celebrate 50 years of matrimony,
Full of joy, precious tears, delicious honey.

Years of ups and downs and laughter,
With handsome sons and gorgeous daughter,
And nine grandkids sheer delight,
When they play and when they fight.

Come along, spread your wings,
Lick your fingers, dance and sing
Perch on Bourke 501 Street,
There's awaiting you a treat.

The day you come with joy driven,
Is Tuesday of December eleven,
From 5 o'clock the drinks on us,
Drown them fast and fear no fuss.

Let's enjoy your gracious presence,
No black tie, and please, no presents,

Just ring Nine Five Zero Nine Seven Eight Five Three
Or email gacohen2003 which is free.

One more thing, your car, no fear,
At the basement park it dear,
And if you can't afford the fee,
Ola and Geoff will guarantee!

To Hashmash

*(Written to my estranged daughter
on the card for her 36th birthday)*

Hope, not despair, springs eternal;
Joy, not anger, is life's kernel.
The brave old horse goes on to breathe
Gallops in tandem, brazing his teeth.

Wishing you Happy Birthday and family bliss,
And from softer lips rush you a kiss;
May the morrow with fragrance dawn
And our hearts to grace drawn.

ODE TO JOUJOU[1]

*(Recited on my wife Judith's 70th birthday at Underbank,
Maree Wray's former farm at Bacchus Marsh)*

We met by chance and warmly courted,
I felt her heart I must no matter win,
We danced and drank and keenly flirted,
And felt the waves of Tonic and Gin.

My life with her is manna from heaven,
When earth is calm and the sky is bright,
My wishes are met sooner than given,
On a sunny day or a moony night.

If love is dutiful in thought and deed,
Hers, throughout, became a creed,
Steadfastly followed the 11th Commandment:
"Honour thy husband each single moment",
And harvest the blessings of amorous devotion,
In quick succession or silent motion.

At 70 she races towards her genial prime,
Busy as a bee, always on time,
Please rise and drink and loudly say,
To my Darling Joujou, "*Happy Birthday*".

And hail Maree, the Princess of Bacchus Marsh,
The Empress of *Underbank*, the champion on the march,
Hostess of warmth and candour and many lavish traits
Bright, proud and daring, a prize to all her mates,

---

1   My term of endearment

Romantic but not easy her heart to discover
The one who wins must be a prince of proven valour
Let's toast Maree and loudly say:
Thank you Maree, here we are joyed to stay!!!

WEDDING RECITAL

*(Honouring Hadas [my wife's first cousin once
removed] and Dr. Michael Schwartsboard)*

The moon in your face smiling,
The stars in your eyes twinkling,
The breeze where now you sit caressing,
And happiness on your faces dancing.

May the divine presence of the *Kotel*[2]
Shine upon you
And may you procreate boys and girls
As lovable as you.

Life's pleasures to each other you'll give,
And to great deeds for *Am Yisrael*[3] you'll live.

And here are my special wishes for you:

*"May your bums stay firm and pert,
And your tummies never head south,
May you never wear big pants,
Or grow unwanted hair,
And, dear Bride and Groom,
If all else fails,
Trust you'd be too sloshed to care"*.

---

2 *Kotel is the sacred Western wall in Jerusalem, Israel.*
3 *Am Yisrael means the People of Israel.*

HAPPY BIRTHDAY, DORON

(My son, on his 45th birthday)

At the age of forty-five,
All your hopes have come to thrive,
May health and joy your future drive
With all loved ones by your side.

Happy Birthday.

Rise up, rise up higher and higher
And reap the rewards you aspire
With all of us who love you

Many Happy Splendid Returns.

HAPPY BIRTHDAY, MICHAEL
(My son, on his 40th Birthday)

Amongst friends, admirers and lovers
You were the star beaming at forty.
May good fortune grace you aplenty
With Cass, Zari, Banjo and kindred others
Around you effusing joy and warmth inbred
Wishing you, dear Michael,

Happy Birthday
And Great many Happy Returns.

With ululating love

ON MY 80ᵀᴴ BIRTHDAY

(Recited at a party celebrating the occasion)

From the serene Rivers of Babylon,
To the undulating Hills of Jerusalem;
From the shy sun of London
And the daring lights of Pigalle
To the meandering waters of the Yarra;
I traversed eighty years of my life
Achieving goals, avoiding strife,
Revelling through beautiful cities
And unmapped alleys
Enjoying the sheen of life
And poetic rallies.

I know not if I'll leave any trail on this earth;
If I do, I know not if it will have any worth
But I love and I dream and I rhyme
A hummingbird on the swing of time
And I treasure the spice and splendour
Of feeling young and looking younger.

And to whom all the credit does belong?
All to *Joujou*[4] who nestled me lifelong,
With the flow of her love and gentle care
And the dishes she creates with artful flair.

How enchanting this gathering by this beautiful lake,
Pleasure to my eyes, Gin and Tonic to my soul;

4 *My term of endearment for my wife Judith*

219

No winter wind shall chill or raging sun shall bake,
The delights of today and my pride in you all.

So, with uplifted heart I welcome you
And thank you for illuminating this day
And set me up, invigorated, to continue
My journey to the last fifth of my holiday!

HAPPY PASSOVER

As joyful as those early years,
When we were young and vibrant
When kisses sounded like thunder
When it was so easy to be fascinated
By the evanescing stars,
The smiling moon,
The sunset
And the legends like
Clark Gable, Ava Gardner, Frank Sinatra.

As joyful as you feel
When any of your wishes
Blossom as a fragrant rose
I so feel wishing you
Happy Passover[5]
And may the DNA of Moses
In Sinai
Become a beautiful rose
Decorating the hearts
Of Israel's
Friends and
Good wishers.

---

5 *The Jewish festival of freedom*

HAPPY BIRTHDAY, TAMI
(On her 70th with husband Rick Olsha)

Happy birthday Tami, happy birthday
May many glorious returns crown your way
With beloved Rick in auspicious whiles
Faces shining with loving smiles.

Shame we'll miss your tea party tonight
But with heart and soul share your delight;
Dear friends you are and so will remain
Clicking together, sunshine or rain.

HAIL MAREE

(Our dear friend Maree Wray, on her 65ᵗʰ Birthday)

Hail Maree reaching a "tender" age
In love each day she turns a glowing page
Candour and passion head her lavish traits
And the way she argues opens the gates.

From yearning to fulfilment
She goes by leaps and bounds
From inclination to decision
She plays the softer sounds

Here's Samson, the prize she long caressed
A prince of joy, gladiator in the nest
Enchanted he rode her humming waves
To reach the shores he stridently craves.

Raise your glasses with me and say
To Dear Maree *Happy Birthday*;
As loving friends we'll always stay
Hail or thunder or come what may.

TO MAREE WRAY AND SAMSON

This evening, while the stars' shine remains bright
Let me recite this poem to enrich your delight.

Chevalier Samson, ambitious, daring quietly candid,
A great achiever in so many ways distinguished;
Saw Maree one day and his sharp eyes twinkled
And like a buzzing arrow his passion sparkled.

With hopes rising and mirthful heart
He steered his course to steal a glance
From her and play his Romeo's part
To win her heart and miss no chance.

She saw him advancing to ring her bell
And the warmth of wine tickled her spices;
He looked so daring, disarmingly swell,
She felt he well deserved all the chances.

Maree was keen to love and be loved
By a Romeo with her passion sweetly folded;
She saw in Samson all virtues nicely shoved
Together with her own divinely moulded.

They partnered and loved each other soon
And flew together to happy shores;
The Angels witnessed their loving boon
And smiling they heard their fancy roars.

You found in each other what glares and gleam
And converted concerns into a wondrous dream;

follow the track of your amorous plays
To the joy and fun of happy nights and days.

Thank you, Maree and Samson, the new stars of night,
For making our sojourn worth the distance in gold;
Almost in a trance we sail on the waves of delight
With all sweet memories in our hearts shall mould.

.

SAM AND PETE KNEW WHAT TO DO FOR THEIR DREAMS TO COME TRUE

Daring Samantha[6] crossed the crowded room
Of rowdy teens at Surfers Paradise;
She faced Peter beaming passion and bloom;
Promptly smitten, he hugged the sweet surprise.

That was in September nineteen ninety-two
And the teenager's love blossomed as they grew.
They travelled, shared values and lots of fun
But footy, cricket and golf were left for Pete to run.

The seeds of love with Noah flowered first,
Jacob followed then Orli quenched the thirst;
The marriage bells rang as Sam and Pete
Reached the summit where they danced and sang:
"Now's the time so let's do it".

Today we see you jubilant husband and wife
And wish you a long, happy and wonderful life.

---

6   *Samantha is the daughter of Maree Wray, my and my wife's dear friend.*

CELEBRATING MY RETIREMENT

*(Addressing family and friends at
the home of my son Michael)*

Today I cull a garland from the flowers
Of your love and friendship as a monument
In my heart for the remaining sunny days
And starry nights of my life in retirement.

This winter day broke blue and bright
And I feel gallant as a nightingale in flight.
I will often meander on the beach
And the gardens without refrain
And inhale the fragrant inspiration
To writing, not working to gain.

And all I ask for is more merry yarns springing
From my loving Joujou with her laughter singing,
And rosy future for my children and their offspring;
For animating G&T and soft music when Bridge I play
And Pinot Noir with dinners and not more weigh.

Thank you, dear Michael, our wonderful host,
We all honour you with a splendid toast
For your graceful, generous welcome and say
You have beautifully elated our day.

■

CONDOLENCES

■

YAFFA, MY DEAR MOTHER (NANA)
(Passed away in 1987)

You lay in the eternal calm
Your soul flying into heaven
Parading the deep love,
The untiring care,
The wise counsel and
The gentle command
You have showered
On me and my seven siblings
Throughout your motherhood
With magic will,
Amazing vitality,
Untiring vigilance
And endearing modesty
With your love flowing like torrents
Into our hearts.

All your tides of life
Rested on our fortunes.

Cruel fate kept me away
From vigil over your bed
To hold your arm,
Gaze on your saintly face and
Arrest the tears I dare not,
With you smiling, shed;
To hold you
In a loving embrace
And say:

"Ayouni *Nana*[1]
your saintly face and shining smile
are my altars;
when I salute your photo
in my study every morning
and feel the flow of your love
in my heart
and the beams of your soul
in my soul.
I love you Nana, I love you
more than words can tell,
more than tears can show.
Your soul will rest in Paradise,
as you might have wished,
forever."

I visited your silent grave;
I placed on it the red roses you loved;
I knelt on both knees

---

1   *Ayouni Nana means "Mother, you are as precious to me as my eyes", an*
    appellation to a person you hold dear.

And kissed it, again and again,
Shedding loving tears,
Remembering the old days in Baghdad
Where you nursed me and my siblings
Shielding us from hazardous slopes
With untiring devotion.

I recalled the songs you cherished,
The friends and family you hosted;
The days I accompanied you to the market
Carrying back the basketful
Of your choice goods.
I recalled the warm welcome
The shopkeepers accorded you and
The delicious dishes you cooked
With envious energy.

We all reach the end of living
Some sighing the hymns of despair,
Others the hope of fresh beginning
In a cradle breathing their mothers' love.
I imagine the days ahead
And see your roses bloom,
Feel your love, like a small sun,
Warming the turrets and vales of my life and
Breathing the perfume
Reeking from your soul
Till ... my heart ... ceases ... to ... beat.

You've departed with greater dignity than
The love and admiration you gained

From all of us siblings
For your tender love and care,
Our life's ornaments.

When the last tide of my life
Runs through my veins
And the windows of light
Are shut in my face,
I will depart eyes closed,
Smiling
Reflecting your
Undying smile.

I ... Love ... you ... Nana
I ... Always ... did

ABRAHAM, MY DEAR BROTHER
(Passed away 18 July, 2001)

Take the oud[2] and gently play the tunes
And softly sing the songs you've savoured;
Yes, make your past splendours shine
And flash upon us, Mum and Dad
And your seven younger siblings,[3]
Your gleeful soul like a star
Shooting brightly along the sky.

Never imagine you as serene dust;
Only a fragrant rose on wayside weeds;
Past the darkness and silence of the grave
I see the glow of life in your face;
I see the great soul that never wavered
Projecting your love, your care and generosity,
Your hearty laughter and engaging presence.

---

2 *Oud is a stringed Middle Eastern musical instrument, similar to a lute*
3 *Ishak, Lily, Daniel, Noor, Gad, Louise and Alon in that order*

You, my loving brother, the Oudist, Tangoist,
Merrymaker, brilliant Hotel[4] Manager;
You've gone to rest where anthems
Of your loving siblings, your wife Rebecca,
Three children and nine grandchildren,[5]
Reverberate as everlasting memorial.
You've reaped our deep love and respect.
Each time I see your radiant face in my study
I feel proud to have been your brother;
I loved you dearly and will do until
My syllables of life flash no more.

---

4   *The (Tigris) River Front Hotel in Baghdad*
5   *Heskel, Emanuel and Daroma and grandchildren Henia Natalie, Joelle
Amy, Ariel Noah, Jordan Abigail, Jamie Elizabeth, Tylor Rose, Amanda
Rachel, Emily Rebecca and Claire Danielle*

TO MY DEAR FRIEND
AHARON NATHAN

*(Condolence on the passing of his
dear wife Sandra, August, 2015)*

What solace can I assemble
For a heart torn asunder;
Words may sound justly idle
'Cause your wound is deep and tender.
Sandra farewelled and none resemble
The treasure she was, the loving wonder.
You stood aloof together
For years and years deep in love
Like the cliffs of Dover
Charming the sky far above;
With sons, kith and kin to treasure
Happy as nightingale and dove.
Tears and smiles and loving touch
Embraced the silence of parting,
Always she cared for you so much
Try to heal the scars remaining.

IN MEMORY OF
PROF. SHMUEL MOREH
(Passed away 22 September 2017)

In the midst of flowering toil
You, my dear lamented old friend,
Went down to your rest, gracing the soil
Of the land you loved and cherished no end.

You loved life with its smiles and tears
And excelled as poet and outstanding scholar;
The praise of your achievements you cannot hear
Time cannot efface nor the seasons wither.

The sad glimmers of goodbyes in your memory shine,
With warm admiration shall for long entwine:
From the banks of the Tigris to University halls
You shone with excellence, no wavering, no falls.

Shame your smiling eyes go under the earth's lid
And the sparks of ebullient talent fade away;
But your shining soul, your loving heart, the works you did
Remain for us bereaving an exquisite array.

The joyful decades of friendship you and I embraced,
The tunes of sorrow my memory within me plays,
And the tears and sighs my grieving heart compressed
Shall roam over my soul for my remaining days.